THE PLAY OF ANTICHRIST

THE PLAY OF ANTICHRIST

Translated, with an Introduction by

JOHN   WRIGHT

THE PONTIFICAL INSTITUTE OF MEDIAEVAL STUDIES
TORONTO, CANADA
1967

Printed by UNIVERSA — WETTEREN — BELGIUM

For Ellen

Acknowledgements

The text of the *Ludus de Antichristo* which I have translated is that edited by Karl Young in his *Drama of the Medieval Church* (Oxford 1962²) 2. 371-387. I want to thank Father T. P. McLaughlin, Editor of *Mediaeval Studies* and Father J. P. Morro, Director of Publications, for the opportunity to publish this work and for the advice and help they gave. Among my teachers here at Indiana University I am especially grateful to Professor Norman T. Pratt, who taught me much of what I know about drama, and Professor James W. Halporn, who first suggested that I translate the play. Finally, I want to thank my wife; her criticism and encouragement have been immeasurably valuable.

J. W.

Bloomington, Indiana,
November 9, 1965.

TABLE OF CONTENTS

PREFACE

Last Emperor

The anonymous *Play of Antichrist* deals with a subject that was of supreme importance to mediaeval authors, artists, and thinkers: the End of the World. Its plot is simple: the Emperor of the Romans (that is, the Holy Roman Emperor) announces his intention to bring the whole world under Roman rule. Despite the opposition of the King of the Franks and the Heathen, this task is accomplished quickly and easily. The Emperor then goes to the Temple at Jerusalem and surrenders his crown and imperial dignity to God. This is the signal for the appearance of Antichrist, who, with the help of his servants the Hypocrites, manages to convince all the kings of the world of his divinity by intimidation, persuasion, and false miracles. His last victims are the Jews, who are convinced that he is the long-awaited Messiah. But as soon as the Jews are seduced, the Prophets Enoch and Elijah appear and save them by showing them the truth. Antichrist is infuriated and has the Prophets and the Jews executed. Finally, as Antichirst summons all the kings and people to worship him, he is destroyed by a thunderbolt from Heaven and the play is over.

The *Play of Antichrist* is the most ambitious mediaeval Latin drama we possess. Its stage represents the whole world, its cast, all humanity. As far as we can tell, its author was a pioneer in many forms of mediaeval Latin rhymed verse and in the use of certain stage techniques, such as allegorical characters and the dumb show. Furthermore, his play is one of the most tightly constructed and best organised in the whole of mediaeval Latin drama.

The unique MS of the play originally came from the Kloster Tegernsee in Bavaria (it is now Munich MS 19411); it is generally assumed that it was written in the twelfth century by a monk from this monastery.[1] In the pages that follow I have tried to show how this playwright combined the legend of the Last Roman Emperor and Antichrist with allusions to the political events of his time (*c.a.* A.D. 1160) to create a play that is one of the best dramatic representations we have of the opinions, the ideas, the hopes, and the fears of the High Middle Ages. It should be emphasised that my account of the background of the play is based upon the generally accepted scholarly opinion concerning the play and its history. My notes will, I hope, make clear those places where some scholars have disagreed with this opinion.

The Latin text I have used to translate the *Play of Antichrist* can be found in Karl Young, *The Drama of the Medieval Church* (Oxford, 1962²) 371-387. In the Appendix I have included a translation of the major source of the play, Adso's *Essay on Antichrist*.

---

[1] E. K. Chambers, *The Mediaeval Stage* (Oxford, 1954⁴) 2. 62n.

INTRODUCTION

LEGENDARY BACKGROUND

The legendary material on which the *Play of Antichrist* is based has a long and complex history; surveying the huge list of material on the subject, one can readily sympathise with the complaint of the author of the *Orologium Sapientiae*: "ther beth so manye bokes and tretees of Antichrist, that this schort lyfe schalle rathere have an ende of anye manne, thanne he may owthere studye hem or rede hem."[1] The account of this legend and its history which follows deals briefly with some of the important highlights in its development; for a more detailed account the reader should consult the bibliography.

The idea of a conflict between God and a powerful adversary personifying and embodying evil is common to many religions; in Judaism its roots undoubtedly go back to the very beginnings of civilisation. For our purposes, however, it will suffice to trace the story only as far back as it was known to mediaeval readers; we may therefore begin with a relatively recent part of the Old Testament, the Book of Daniel. Although for most modern readers this book is memorable mainly for its accounts of the Handwriting on the Wall and the Den of Lions,[2] Christian commentators from the earliest times were particularly interested

---

[1] Quoted by L. U. Lucken, *Antichrist and the Prophets of Antichrist in the Chester Cycle* (Washington, 1940) viii. In addition to Lucken's work, my account is based on Wilhelm Bousset, *The Antichrist Legend*, tr. A. H. Keane (London, 1896); Norman Cohn, *The Pursuit of the Millennium* (Fairlawn, N. J., 1957); and *The Holy Bible: A Translation from the Latin Vulgate in the Light of the Hebrew and Greek Originals*, tr. R. A. Knox (London, 1955). Good bibliographies can be found in Lucken 151-156 and Cohn 430-462.

[2] These aspects were by no means neglected by mediaeval readers either; they formed the basis for the magnificent French Latin *Play of Daniel*, roughly contemporary with the *Play of Antichrist*.

in a number of dreams or visions related in chapters 7-12. In the first dream the prophet Daniel sees four horrible beasts who overcome each other one by one; the last is himself overcome by a white-gowned Judge. Daniel is troubled, and the dream is interpreted historically for him by "one that stood by" (7.16), who says in part:

> ... and after these [kings] another shall rise, more powerful yet, and three of them shall bite the dust. Boastfully he shall challenge the most High, and do his servants despite; calendar and ordinance he shall think to set aside; for a space of time, and for twice as long, and for half as long, he must needs have his way. Then assize shall be held on him, and all his power be taken away, crushed down and forgotten for ever (7.24-26).

The second vision also consists of a number of beasts; from the horns of one of them a little horn springs, which overcomes "the armies of heaven itself" (8.10) and causes "a cessation of sacrifice" which will last, Daniel is told, "two thousand three hundred days" (8.13-14). (This last figure can also be interpreted to mean 1,150 days,[3] or about three and a half years, as can the strange references to a "space of time" quoted above; this, as we shall see, was the interpretation mediaeval commentators preferred.) The vision is interpreted for Daniel by the angel Gabriel, who says of the little horn:

> ... the world shall go from bad to worse, till a new king comes to the throne, brazen-faced, a master of riddles. Great power shall he wield ... making havoc beyond belief, thriving and prospering .... And at last with the Prince of princes he shall try conclusions; no human hand shall it be that crushes him down at last (8.23-25).

Daniel has other visions, but the final vision of the Book is of the greatest interest for the story of Antichrist. Here a man "clad all in linen" (10.5), with shining face and burning eyes,

---

[3] Because of the two daily sacrifices in the Temple; see Knox's note to this verse.

gives Daniel a detailed prophecy of future history, ending with
the final king,

> ... a man little thought of; royal investiture he has none,
> yet see how stealthy his approach, what shifts he uses to win
> a throne! Down go strong armies, crushed before him ...
> (11.21-22) And now ... he shall vent his spleen against the
> holy covenant in good earnest. The forsakers of that
> covenant have not escaped his eye, and there are willing
> hands a many to help him profane the inviolable sanctuary,
> daily sacrifice annulling, spreading defilement and deso-
> lation there .... (11.30-31) As for the king, he shall have
> all his own way; in his pride, he will think himself a match
> for any god, even of that God boast himself a rival, who is
> above all gods. And still he shall thrive; vengeance is not
> yet ready to overtake him; doom shall come when doom must
> (11.36). See where he sets up his royal pavilion betwixt sea
> and sea on yonder noble hill, yonder sacred hill; reaches
> its very summit, and none brings aid! (11.45)
>
> Time, then, that Michael should be up and doing; Michael,
> that high lord who is guardian of thy race. Distress shall
> then be, such as never was since the world began; and in
> that hour of distress thy fellow-countrymen shall win
> deliverance, all whose names are found written when the
> record lies open. Many shall wake, that now lie sleeping
> in the dust of earth, some to enjoy life everlasting, some to
> be confronted for ever with their disgrace (12.1-2).

I have quoted at length from these prophecies in order to show
how much of the Antichrist eschatology can be traced back to
this single, relatively early, source. Modern commentators
generally agree that these verses refer to Antiochus Epiphanes
(reigned 176-164 B.C.), the Seleucid king of Syria who defiled
the Temple at Jerusalem and who was eventually driven out in
the revolt of the Maccabees.[4] Whether this interpretation is
true or not is unimportant for our purposes; to early and
mediaeval Christian commentators the verses referred to the

---

4 See Knox's note on 7.27, *et passim*. (Knox finds many difficulties with
this interpretation.)

adversary of God they called Antichrist,[5] and in fact we can
find in these verses almost all the important facets of his story.
To sum up: according to Daniel, this adversary will be stealthy
and deceitful as well as powerful and destructive[6] (this dicho-
tomy causes confusion in some later accounts, but the author of
the *Play of Antichrist* handles it neatly by having Antichrist
exhibit different facets of his character to the different kings he
overcomes); he will challenge God and proclaim himself God's
equal; he will defile the Temple; he will reign with universal
success for three and a half years; finally he will set up his
pavilion on a certain "noble hill" (later commentators decided
this was to be Mount Olivet), at which point he will be destroyed
by the Archangel Michael and the Last Judgment will follow.
Very little of substance besides this was added to the legend of
Antichrist himself by later writers.

One important point did remain, however: the identification
of the nameless adversary found in these prophecies with the
opponent of Christ, the opposite of Christ who was to be called
Antichrist. Mediaeval commentators found their major source
for this identification in the words of Christ Himself. The
Gospels[7] report that in a private conversation with His disciples
on Mount Olivet, Christ warned of false announcements of the
End of the World and then went on, mentioning the prophecies
of Daniel (Matt. 24.15), to describe the true End. The prophecy
reads in part:

> ... there will be distress then such as has not been since
> the beginning of the world, and can never be again. There
> would have been no hope left for any human creature, if the

---

[5] The notes to the Appendix included at the end of this work will
give some examples of how Daniel's visions were interpreted by St. Jerome
and the later commentator Haymo of Halberstadt. (The actual name
"Antichrist" is a New Testament addition; see below.)

[6] Karl Young (*The Drama of the Medieval Church* [Oxford, 1933, 1962]
2. 370) feels that Antichrist's stealth was an aspect added by the
Christians, but a close reading of the Daniel passages I have quoted does
not bear this out. This aspect was certainly emphasised by Christian
commentators, however.

[7] I quote the version of Matthew because this was the one most used
by the mediaeval commentators.

number of those days had not been cut short; but those days will be cut short, for the sake of the elect. At such a time, if a man tells you, See, here is Christ, or, See, he is there, do not believe him. There will be false Christs and false prophets, who will rise up and shew great signs and wonders, so that if it were possible, even the elect would be deceived. Mark well, I have given you warning of it (24.21-25).

Particularly because Christ Himself cited Daniel while making this prophecy, later commentators felt justified in connecting His words to the account of God's adversary in the Book of Daniel. A number of important facets were thus added to the Antichrist eschatology: as well as being the warlike conquerer he was in Daniel, the adversary (he does not yet have a name) is definitely identified as a persecutor of the elect (i.e., the followers of Christ); false miracles will be a part of his deception; and he will claim to be the Christ.

The vast complexities as well as the beauties of the Book of the Apocalypse are well known; fortunately it is unnecessary for our purpose to delve too deeply into its confusing narrative to discover what it had to add to the Antichrist legend. Most important was the account of the Two Witnesses. It is stated that

> ... the Gentiles ... will tread the holy city under foot for a space of forty-two months [another reference to the three-and-a-half-year reign of God's adversary]. Meanwhile I will give the power of prophecy to my two witnesses; for twelve hundred and sixty days [again, three and a half years] they shall prophesy, dressed in sackcloth; these are the two olive-trees, the two candlesticks thou knowest of, that stand before him who is Lord of the earth[8] (11.2-4). Then, when they have borne me witness to the full, the beast which comes up out of the abyss will make war on them, and defeat and kill them. (11.7) Then, after three and a half days, by God's gift the breath of life entered into them, and they rose to their feet ... (11.11).

8 The imagery refers to Zach. 4.3, 11-14 (Knox).

These two witnesses, who are to expose God's adversary and then be temporarily defeated by him, were generally identified by later commentators with the Old Testament prophets Enoch and Elijah.[9] Elijah's presence is not surprising: he plays a large and memorable role in the Old Testament (3 and 4 Kings); he is there reported as being taken up, presumably alive, into Heaven ("... all at once ... a flaming chariot appeared, drawn by flaming horses, and Elias went up on a whirlwind into heaven." 4 Kings 2.11); his return was expected even in pre-Christian times (Malachias 4.5: "I will send Elias to be your prophet") and especially in Christ's time.[10] Enoch, on the other hand, though called "God's close friend" (Gen. 5.22), is dealt with in only five short verses in the Book of Genesis; his major achievement there is the begetting of Mathusala. To be sure, the end of his life is reported in an ambiguous way (5.24: "God took him to himself, and he was seen no more") which suggests a possible assumption into Heaven, and which offers an *a priori* reason for his eventual return. But it is difficult to see why he should be coupled with the far more famous Elijah, especially since Elijah's partner in the Gospels (see, for example, the account of the Transfiguration in Matt. 17) is usually Moses.[11] The answer to this difficulty possibly lies in the existence of an apocryphal Book of Enoch, generally assigned to the second and first centuries B.C.[12] Besides the usual denunciations of evil found in prophetic literature, this book contains a memorable prophecy of the End of the World, which was well enough known in early Christian times to be referred to and quoted in the General Epistle of Jude

[9] I am using, here and in the translation of the play, the forms of the names of the Prophets most familiar in English. In the Vulgate, and hence in Knox's translation, the names are given as Henoch and Elias.

[10] See, for example, Matt. 11.14, 17.10-12, 27.47, 49.

[11] The difficulty of the presence of Enoch, and in fact the whole question of why there were two witnesses rather than one, is illustrated by the fact that Bousset, despite his exhaustive researches, is forced to leave the question open (210-211). The ante-Nicene commentator Ireneus appears to have been the first to have identified the Witnesses as Enoch and Elijah; see Lucken 57.

[12] The book is translated in R. H. Charles, ed., *The Apocrypha and Pseudepigrapha of the Old Testament in English* (Oxford, 1913) 2, 168-281.

(Jude 14-15). The combination of the popularity of the Book of
Enoch and the theory of Enoch's assumption seem to have been
enough to earn Enoch his important place in the Antichrist
eschatology.

The second major addition made to the legend by the
Apocalypse was the Mark of the Beast. The text reads:

> All alike, little and great, rich and poor, free men and
> slaves, must receive a mark from him on their right hands,
> or on their foreheads, and none might buy or sell, unless he
> carried this mark, which was the beast's name, or the number
> that stands for his name (Apoc. 13.16-17).

Earlier in the Apocalypse (cf. 6.6, and Knox's note) it had been
stated that one facet of the End of the World would be a
famine; the Mark of the Beast described here is a sign that
enabled men to "buy and sell," and thus survive this famine.
But the two accounts, of the famine and the mark, are so far
apart in the Apocalypse that their connection was obscure to
mediaeval commentators, who came to regard the mark simply
as a symbol of submission to Antichrist.[13] The existence of this
symbol was particularly fortunate for the author of the *Play of
Antichrist*; with it he had a concrete dramatic method of
indicating the exact moment when each of his characters fell to
Antichrist.

The name "Antichrist" itself is a late accretion to the
eschatology. A Greek construction (*anti-* "opposite, against"
+*chrístos* "the annointed"), it appears only in the Epistles of
John (1 Jn. 2.18, 4.3; 2 Jn. 7); elsewhere in the New Testament
the adversary is referred to in such general terms as "the son of
perdition" (2 Thess. 2.3; translated by Knox, more accurately
but less traditionally, as "[he who is] destined to inherit
perdition").[14]

With the addition of his name we have now covered the main
points of the eschatology of Antichrist himself: his opposition to

[13] See Bousset 200-202.
[14] Other interpretations of the *anti-* prefix, such as "resembling," are
also possible; see Lucken 12-13.

God, his deceitfulness and power, his three-and-a-half-year reign, the mark he places on his victims, the opposition he faces in the prophets Enoch and Elijah, his claim to be the Messiah, his tent on Mount Olivet, and his final destruction at the hands of God.[15] In the centuries immediately following the death of Christ, the scriptural sources we have examined were taken along with the oral tradition and a vast number of apocryphal gospels, prophetic works, and apocalypses in various languages; all this material was sifted, expanded, and explicated by early Christian homilists and Biblical commentators.[16] The Antichrist eschatology as a whole, however, remained substantially in the form outlined above. But an important part of it which appears to be its last major accretion remains to be examined. This is the tradition of the last and all-powerful Emperor of the World whose universal triumph was to precede the advent of Antichrist.

Prediction and speculation regarding the Last Days became less popular among Christians as the Catholic Church became more powerful, and in fact belief in the Millennium was officially condemned at the Council of Ephesus in 431.[17] But two setbacks suffered by orthodox Christianity, one before this council and one after, led to widespread acceptance of the prediction of a future warrior-emperor who, by persuasion and

[15] To mediaeval commentators and the *Antichrist* playwright, who of course regarded the Scriptures as a unified whole, the notion of a historically developing Antichrist would be completely foreign. I have used the historical method in tracing the eschatology simply to give some order to my narrative of it.

[16] Of the commentators (besides obvious choices like Jerome and Augustine) Bousset mentions, among others, St. Cyril of Jerusalem, pseudo-Hippolytus, St. Ephrem (and pseudo-Ephrem), Philip the Solitary, pseudo-Chrysostom, Ireneus, and Lactantius. The apocryphal material includes "Apocalypses of Peter" in Arabic, Syriac, and Ethiopic, Apocalypses of Ezra and Zephaniah, and the Book of Clement. As far as I have been able to discover, as yet no broadly based scholarly consensus on the development of the eschatology in this period exists; in fact, the study can still be said to be in its infancy. I have therefore avoided any attempt to summarise in a few sentences the development of the Antichrist legend in the early Christian period. There is a list of pre-thirteenth-century treatments of the Antichrist theme in Migne's *Patrologia latina* 219, 49-52 and 220, 265-308; see Lucken 2.

[17] Cohn 14.

force of arms, would some day destroy the enemies of orthodoxy throughout the world.

The first of these setbacks was the accession of the Emperor Constantius II (son of Constantine, under whom Christianity became the official religion of the Empire), who had accepted the Arian heresy. For ten years (A.D. 340-350) Constantius had ruled the eastern half of the Empire, while his brother, Constans I, an orthodox Christian, ruled in the west. But when Constans was assassinated in 350, Constantius became sole emperor. The distress orthodox Christians felt at this led to the production of the "Tiburtine Sibyl," a set of prophecies cast in the Sibylline form which by this time had become traditional with pagans, Jews, and Christians alike.[18] The *Tiburtina* *last* predicts the triumphant return of Constans for a reign that will *Eupor* last more than a century. It will be a time of comfort and abundance: the exact prices (all of them presumably very low) of various food products are happily enumerated. Constans will defeat the pagans; the Jews will be converted to Christianity; finally the Emperor will go to Jerusalem and offer up his crown to God. After this Antichrist will come; his brief reign follows the outline given above. After his destruction comes the End of the World.

The second major setback to Christianity was the coming of Islam. This produced another collection of "oracles," originally written in the late seventh century for the Christians of Syria, who were now in the unhappy position of living under the rule (however tolerant it might have been) of the followers of another religion.[19] The collection was falsely ascribed to the fourth-century bishop Methodius of Patara and is therefore known as

18 For a brief account of the *Tiburtina* see Cohn 15-16. The text is in Ernst Sackur, *Sibyllinische Texte und Forschungen* (Halle, 1898) 177-187; his text, with a German translation, is reprinted in Alfons Kurfess, *Sibyllinische Weissagungen* (Munich, 1951) 262-279. The expectation of the return of various emperors was by this time a commonplace; the earliest Roman emperor whose return was joyfully anticipated was, amazingly enough, Nero (see Suetonius, *Nero* 57).
19 See Cohn 16-17. The text of the *Pseudo-Methodius* is also in Sackur (59-96).

the *Pseudo-Methodius*. It describes the devastation wrought on
the Christians by the followers of Islam, here called "Ishmaelites," and predicts the re-awakening of a long-sleeping Emperor
who will defeat the "Ishmaelites" and eventually give up his
crown in Jerusalem; the usual advent of Antichrist and Last
Judgment follow.

Despite the official opposition noted above, millennial prophecies, and the *Tiburtina* and *Pseudo-Methodius* in particular,
were immensely popular; both works were copied and circulated
widely throughout the Middle Ages and even into the Renaissance.[20] The story of the Last Emperor semed to have scriptural
sanction, for in his Second Epistle to the Thessalonians, St. Paul,
warning the Thessalonians not to expect the End of the World
immediately, had stated, in reference to the Antichrist,

> "At present there is a power (you know what I mean) which
> holds him [Antichrist] in check, so that he may not shew
> himself before the time appointed to him; meanwhile, the
> conspiracy of revolt is already at work; only, he who checks
> it now will be able to check it, until he is removed from the
> enemy's path. Then it is that the rebel will shew himself ...."
> (2.6-8).

A modern commentator suggests that "the power which holds
evil in check and defers the appearance of Antichrist may be a
human influence, or perhaps that of St. Michael or some other
angel";[21] but earlier commentators where much less modest and
circumspect about their identifications.[22] The "power," they felt,
was the Roman Empire, and when it had ended with the Last
Emperor's surrender of his crown at Jerusalem, the reign of
Antichrist would come. What we generally call the "fall of the
Roman Empire" in 476 did not daunt them; for a while they
looked to the Eastern Empire, until the revival of the Western
Empire under Charlemagne gave them new fuel with which to
feed their hopes.

---

[20] See Cohn 17-18.
[21] Knox's note on 2 Thess. 2.6.
[22] See, for example, Adso's treatment of this passage in the Appendix.

During the Middle Ages there were many restatements of the legend of the Last Roman Emperor and Antichrist, and in fact they continue down to our own time.[23] But for the purpose of explaining the *Play of Antichrist*, the last and most important version is the *Essay on Antichrist* (*Libellus de Antichristo*) written by the French monk Adso in the tenth century for Gerberga, Queen of France. Although it never quite supplanted the *Tiburtina* and the *Pseudo-Methodius*, the *Essay* was immensely popular; it was copied and distributed widely and came to be the standard source for information on the Last Days.[24] Because the *Essay* is almost universally regarded as the main source of the *Play of Antichrist*,[25] I have included an annotated translation of it as an appendix to this work. It is therefore unnecessary to summarise its contents, which at this point should be familiar to the reader anyway: they include the prediction of the Last Roman Emperor, the advent of Antichrist, his temporary triumph and eventual destruction at the hands of God. In a subsequent part of this introduction I have tried to show how the author of the *Play of Antichrist* has taken this huge body of material, which was presented in a particularly confused form in Adso, his immediate source, and organised it into the most imposing and awesome play to be found in the mediaeval Latin drama.

[23] For an outline (with a brief general bibliography) of some of the millennial prophecy which followed the *Play of Antichrist*, see Marjorie Reeves, "Joachimist Influences on the Idea of a Last World Emperor," *Traditio* 17 (1961) 323-370.

[24] It was used, for example, as the main source for the Antichrist story in Otto of Freising's account of the End of the World in his universal history, *The Two Cities* (tr. C. C. Mierow; Columbia University Records of Civilization [9], New York, 1928). The text of the *Essay*, the full title of which is *Epistola Adsonis ad Gerbergam reginam de ortu et tempore Antichristi*, has been authoritatively edited by Sackur, 104-113. This text is reproduced in Young 2. 496-500. The text in Migne 101, 129 ff. is very poor.

[25] See E. K. Chambers, *The Mediaeval Stage* (Oxford, 1954[4]) 2, 63-64; Young 2, 390; and compare the references in both works. But see also note 54 in the next part of this introduction.

HISTORICAL BACKGROUND

From the above account of the legend of Antichrist and the Last Roman Emperor, the reader of the *Play of Antichrist* can easily see that almost all of the substance of the play is taken from the legend. The search for reflections of real history in the play is dangerous, because it is so simple and elemental that its events could easily be twisted to suit the history of almost any period in the Middle Ages. But the researches of political and literary historians have made it possible to discuss with reasonable certainty a number of historical references in the play.[1] These are concentrated in its first part, which describes the ascendancy of the Last Roman Emperor; to understand them we must have an outline of certain important contemporary events in the history of the Holy Roman Empire.

The *Play of Antichrist* is generally dated around the year 1160,[2] an important year for the Emperor Frederick I Barbarossa of Hohenstaufen and his heroic but futile attempt to construct a unified empire out of the dozens of autonomous states and principalities of Germany and northern Italy. The Imperial Electors had chosen Frederick emperor in 1152, at a time when anarchy reigned in Germany and Eastern Europe and neglect had atrophied the imperial authority among the wealthy city-states of Italy.[3] Upon his accession Frederick immediately

---

[1] The following account is based upon the generally accepted opinion regarding the politics of the play. Some scholars disagree, at times violently, with this opinion; I have tried to indicate these disagreements in the notes to this section.

[2] This date is arrived at on grounds that will be discussed later (in particular, the falling-out between the Emperor and the King of France, and Gerhoh of Reichersberg's *De investigatione Antichristi*). See Karl Young, *The Drama of the Medieval Church* (Oxford, 1933, 1962[2]) 2. 393; E. K. Chambers, *The Mediaeval Stage* (Oxford, 1954[4]) 2, 64; and Karl Langosch, *Politische Dichtung um Kaiser Friedrich Barbarossa* (Berlin, 1943) 284-285.

[3] For an outline of Frederick's activities in Germany see A. L. Poole, "Frederick Barbarossa and Germany," *Cambridge Medieval History* 5

proclaimed and subsequently enforced a land peace forbidding private war throughout Germany. He mediated (although without permanent success) a dispute for the throne of Denmark, and forced recognition of his suzerainty on the monarchs of the recently christianised territories of Poland, Hungary, and Bohemia.

Had Frederick been content to concentrate his efforts on Germany, his strength, force of character, intelligence, and instinctive knowledge of the use of political and military power might well have gone a long way to create for his country the kind of permanent unity which was being brought to France and England by his contemporaries, Louis VII and Henry II. But unfortunately for Germany, Frederick possessed a streak of romanticism which was to help make his reign "one of the most magnificent failures in history."[4] He was an avid student of history, very conscious of his position as the successor of Constantine and Charlemagne.[5] This, and his desire to re-establish the imperial claims of his more immediate predecessors, led him to spend most of his reign wasting the resources of his nation in a futile attempt to recreate that Roman Empire to which he added the sobriquet "Holy."[6] This effort was concen-

(Cambridge, 1926) 381-412, and Langosch 7-28. The *Gesta Frederici,* a contemporary account of the earlier events of the Emperor's reign, was written at his request by his historian uncle: Otto of Freising and Rahewin, *The Deeds of Frederick Barbarossa,* tr. C. C. Mierow (Columbia Universty Records of Civilization, 49, New York, 1953). Rahewin, Otto's secretary, completed the biography, which hereafter will be referred to as *Gesta,* after Otto's death.

4 P. J. Knapke, *Frederick Barbarossa's Conflict with the Papacy: A Problem of Church and State* (Universitas Catholica Americae Studia Theologica, 55, Washington, 1939) 116.

5 See *Gesta* 4.86 and the letter from Frederick to Otto prefixed to the *Gesta.* Frederick's romanticism and historical sense were of course not the only reasons for his attempt to unify Germany and Italy under the Empire; the inherited anomaly of the position of the Holy Roman Emperor was partly to blame.

6 James Viscount Bryce, *The Holy Roman Empire* (London, 1963³) 196. This title is a true indication of the spirit in which Frederick approached the task of restoring the Empire; its note of theocracy suggests in part the origin of Frederick's conflict with the papacy.

trated in northern Italy, where the growing nationalism and economic power of the cities which later formed the Lombard League doomed Frederick's notion of imperial sovereignty from the start.[7] Again and again he would beat down the Lombard cities, only to see them rise again, sometimes literally from rubble and ashes, the moment his attention was diverted. Sometimes events in Germany would demand his presence. At one time disease among his troops forced a humiliating retreat. The final end to Frederick's hopes came with the Battle of Legnano in 1176, in which the Imperial Army was crushed by the recently formed Lombard League. The subsequent peace of Venice ended the practical power of the Empire in northern Italy.

But Frederick's fortunes in Italy had their high points as well, and one of these was in 1158, two years before the composition of the *Play of Antichrist*. In this year, his position strengthened by recent victories over the Lombard cities, Frederick summoned the Italians to the Diet of Roncaglia.[8] Here he judged disputes, set up imperial representatives called *podestà* for all the cities, outlawed private war, and re-established forgotten imperial prerogatives.[9] "At that moment the authority of the Empire appeared absolute in Italy and as if it were to last for ever."[10] Despite some difficulties in the next two years, Frederick's position regarding the Italian cities in 1160 (the year of our play) was still one of almost unchallenged imperial sovereignty.

Frederick's ambitions in Italy were the most immediate cause of the second great problem of his reign, his conflict with the papacy.[11] Relations between Pope and Emperor began auspiciously in 1153 with the Treaty of Constance, entered into by Frederick and Pope Eugenius III.[12] The Emperor promised to

---

[7] For a brief account of Frederick's activities in Italy see Ugo Balzani, "Frederick Barbarossa and the Lombard League," *Cambridge Medieval History* 5 (Cambridge, 1926) 413-453.

[8] *Gesta* 4.1-10.

[9] Knapke 50.

[10] Balzani, "Lombard League" 427.

[11] Ugo Balzani, *The Popes and the Hohenstaufen* (New York, 1889) 48 ff.

[12] Knapke 28.

help the Pope subdue republican rebels in the city of Rome, and the Pope in turn promised him general assistance and the all-important imperial crown. In 1155, Frederick placated the new pope, an Englishman named Nicholas Breakspear who took the name of Adrian IV, by handing over to his custody Arnold of Brescia, a reformer who had been stirring up rebellion in Rome. But in his first face-to-face meeting with Adrian he refused to act as the Pope's squire by holding his stirrup — a bit of symbolic ceremonial of the sort that was taken very seriously in the Middle Ages.[13] He soon relented, performed the ceremony, and received the imperial crown in Rome on June 18, 1155, but it was clear that, with the combination of his imperial ambitions and his sense of his place in history (for he was well aware of the great power that Constantine and Charlemagne had exercised over the Church), he intended to remain independent of the papacy and in fact to control it if he could.[14] That very year a quarrel broke out when Adrian made a treaty with the King of Sicily — an act which Frederick, who claimed Sicily as part of the Empire, felt violated the implied terms of the Constance treaty he had made with Adrian's predecessor. He therefore refused the Pope's request to help an Archbishop who had been captured by some German knights. Adrian's letter of protest at this added fuel to the flames by an ambiguous use of the word *beneficia*; the word could mean "favors," but Frederick understood it as "benefice," and maintained that Adrian was trying to claim the Empire as a papal fief. The papal envoys were immediately dismissed, and the Emperor sent an angry letter to the bishops of Germany describing the alleged insult.[15] A letter of explanation from the Pope settled the argument, but only temporarily. It flared up again over the old question of who was to appoint bishops to imperial dioceses. This controversy, supposedly settled two generations earlier by the Concordat of Worms, grew hotter and hotter; Adrian and

---

13 *Ibid.* 33-34.
14 Perhaps Frederick's contact with Byzantium as a young man on the Second Crusade contributed to his belief in absolutism and caesaropapism. See Knapke 21n.
15 *Gesta* 3.11.

Frederick took to trading subtle insults in their correspondence (the Emperor addressed the Pope as *tu* instead of *vos*, for example).[16] Finally Adrian sent letters to the Lombard cities urging them to revolt; by 1159, he was openly supporting the Lombards and had agreed to excommunicate Frederick within forty days when the conflict was interrupted, but not ended, by Adrian's death on September 1.[17]

A new pope had to be elected, and on September 7, 1159, the College of Cardinals convened. The majority voted for Roland, an anti-imperialist cardinal who had been one of the envoys during the *beneficia* crisis (and who had, in fact, incensed that situation by asking at the time, "From whom then does he [the Emperor] have the empire, if not from our lord the pope?").[18] But the two-thirds majority rule for papal elections did not yet exist,[19] and a vociferous minority of cardinals held out for Octavian, the imperialist candidate. A ridiculous scene ensued, with both candidates carrying on a tug-of-war for the papal *pallium;* the anti-imperialists were eventually put to flight by a timely incursion of imperial soldiers. Roland and Octavian excommunicated each other, and a schism that was to last twenty years was on.

It is uncertain whether Frederick had anything to do with the travesty of this election; at any rate, on his own initiative and citing the examples of such imperial predecessors as Constantine and Charlemagne, he summoned a council to decide the question which met at Pavia on February 5, 1160.[20] It was attended

---

[16] *Ibid.* 4.21.

[17] Knapke 55.

[18] *Gesta* 3.10.

[19] It was adopted shortly afterward under Pope Alexander III as a result of the controversy surrounding this election. The partisans of the imperialist candidate based their case in this election on the doctrine that an election was decided by the *major et sanior pars* ("greater and sounder part") of those voting. For a discussion see Alan Gewirth, *Marsilius of Padua: The Defender of Peace* 1 (Columbia University Records of Civilization 46, New York, 1951) 182-199.

[20] When the Council convened, Frederick said to the bishops: "... I know that, by virtue of my office and the dignity of the empire, the authority to convoke councils (especially in such great perils of the

almost only by imperial prelates, and its decision was a foregone
conclusion. Roland, who had taken the name of Alexander III,
was accused of treason against the Empire, and Octavian was
declared pope as Victor IV. Alexander, declaring that the Pope
alone had the right to summon a council, excommunicated
Frederick and the break was complete. As in the case of the
Lombard League, this conflict too ended in defeat for Frederick;
in fact, the stubbornness, idealism, and political skill of Pope
Alexander III was a major factor in paving the way for what
has been called the "papal monarchy" of Pope Innocent III.[21]

The schism between Alexander III and Frederick's antipopes
led to another problem for the Emperor, one which was not very
serious in the long run but which must have seemed quite
important in 1160. The kings of France and England had always
vaguely recognised the primacy of the Emperor among the
monarchs of Christian Europe.[22] Naturally Frederick was eager
to get their support for Victor as pope. But on July 22, 1160,
ignoring the decision of the Emperor's Pavia council, they met at
Toulouse and decided to accept Alexander.[23] Relations between
the two sides grew strained; Frederick's repeated efforts in
Victor's behalf met with no response. In 1163, at the Council of
Tours, France and England reiterated their support of Alexander.[24] The difficulty was solved, however, when Frederick later
yielded and joined the other monarchs in accepting Alexander;
by 1187, he had formed a close alliance with the new King
Philip Augustus of France.[25]

It is necessary to take a brief glance at the situation at this
time in the East, and particularly in the Holy Land, since this

Church) is vested in me — for it is recorded that the emperors Constantine and Theodosius and Justinian also, and in more recent times Charles
the Great and Otto did so ...." *Gesta* 4.74.

21 Knapke 89. (Knapke does not, however, use the popular term "papal
monarchy" to describe Innocent's reign.)

22 The language of a letter of 1157 from Henry II of England is very
obsequious: "We lay before you our kingdom ... that in all respects your
imperial will may be done." *Gesta* 3.7.

23 Knapke 68.

24 *Ibid.* 72.

25 Poole 397.

area plays an important part in the *Play of Antichrist*.[26] The
First Crusade had succeeded largely because of the disunity and
turmoil which prevailed over the Near East when the Crusaders
had arrived. Since that time, however, the Moslems were
becoming more unified and powerful. The Second Crusade (1147-
49), so movingly preached by St. Bernard, had been a dismal
failure and every Christian in the West knew it.[27] By 1160,
Baldwin III, King of Jerusalem, though a great leader and a
victor in a number of important battles, was largely playing a
defensive game. The powerful Byzantine *Basileus*, Manuel
Comnenus, was trying to maintain the balance of power as
"a kind of arbiter of Near Eastern politics."[28] The fact that
he and the leaders of the Latin Crusader states found it possible
to form alliances with Moslems as well as Christians was a
constant source of surprise and disillusionment to visiting
Westerners and new Crusaders. Among the Moslems, the
powerful Nur-ad-Din was keeping the Latin states under
constant pressure. But this pressure was just a hint of what was
to come under the future Moslem leader Saladin (1169-89), who
defeated the Third Crusade and reconquered all of Palestine.[29]

To the eyes of an imperialist writer like the *Antichrist* playwright,[30] the world situation in 1160 might look something like
this: he would see in Frederick Barbarossa a powerful emperor

[26] For fuller accounts see C. L. Kingsford, "The Kingdom of Jerusalem," *Cambridge Medieval History* 5 (Cambridge, 1926) 300-319 and
M. W. Baldwin, "The Latin States under Baldwin III and Amalric I,
1143-1174," *A History of the Crusades* 1, K. M. Setton, ed. (Philadelphia,
1955) 528-562.

[27] V. G. Berry, "The Second Crusade," *Ibid.* 463-512.

[28] Baldwin, "Latin States" 530.

[29] Sir Hamilton A. R. Gibb, "The Rise of Saladin, 1169-1189," *ibid.*
563-589 and M. W. Baldwin, "The Decline and Fall of Jerusalem, 1174-
1189," *ibid.* 590-621.

[30] The strongest opposition to this opinion regarding the political
position of the playwright is to be found in Eduard Michaelis's article,
"Zum Ludus de Antichristo," *Zeitschrift für deutsches Altertum* 54 (1913)
61-87. He states very emphatically that "politische spitzen sind im L de
AX [i.e., *Ludus de Antichristo*] nicht vorhanden" (p. 81); he feels that
the play was written mainly in support of the ethical and theological
position of St. Bernard.

who gave good promise of returning the Empire to the heights it had reached under Otto I and Charlemagne (the defeat at Legnano, of course, no one could foresee). He would see a pope, Victor IV, completely subservient to the Emperor in the best caesaro-papist tradition (the eventual victory of Alexander would also be difficult to predict). He would see the King of France, and his powerful vassal the King of England, wickedly refusing to accept imperial authority in the matter of the papal schism (he could not know of the future alliance between France and the Empire). And finally, perhaps with the memory of the disastrous crusade of eleven years before still fresh in his mind, he would see a beleaguered Holy Land which clearly needed the strong hand of a crusading monarch to rescue it (no one could know that the Third Crusade a generation later would lead to fresh disaster and to Frederick's ignominious death by accidental drowning). We shall now see how such a view of the international scene influenced the composition of the *Play of Antichrist*.

After the introductory songs sung by Gentilitas, Synagoga, and Ecclesia, the real action of the play opens with the Emperor of the Romans asserting his sovereignty over all the world. As we have seen above, a German patriot writing in 1160 would have ample grounds to see in Frederick Barbarossa an Emperor whose power and prestige might lead to the hope that he would accomplish this tremendous task. His political skill had already ended the anarchy which prevailed in Germany at the time of his accession, while his armed strength had brought the rebellious Italian communes to heel. The legendary material with which the *Antichrist* playwright was working claimed that a Roman Emperor would one day subdue the world. What better candidate than Frederick, who had already been so succesful? Of course, he was at the moment having his difficulties with the insubordinate King of France,[31] who refused to recognise

---

[31] It is possible that the playwright omitted the King of England because he was nominally the vassal of the King of France, or perhaps simply because England was so remote from his world. But more probably he was just simplifying the drama by allowing the "King of the Franks" to stand for all western European monarchs.

the man who (in our playwright's eyes) was the true Pope.
Therefore in creating the character of the "King of the Franks,"
he made him stubborn and rebellious, though contrite enough
(as the leaders of the defeated Italian cities no doubt were) when
faced with the reality of the Emperor's military might.[32]

The playwright puts into the Emperor's mouth certain striking
grounds for claiming sovereignty over the King of the Franks
and the other kings. The Emperor tells his messengers:

The writings of historians tell us
That once the whole world was a Roman fief. (49-50)

and goes on to say that although lazy emperors of later times
relaxed their hold on this possession, he has now come to reclaim
it. These lines reflect an important intellectual movement which
was at its peak at the time the *Play of Antichrist* was composed
and in which the Emperor Frederick was vitally interested. This
was the revival of Roman law. Since to my knowledge this play
has never been brought forward as evidence of this movement,
it might be worthwhile to examine more closely the question of
Roman law and its effect on the position of the Holy Roman
Emperor.[33]

The basic text of the Roman law was the *Corpus Juris Civilis*,
codified by the sixth-century Roman Emperor Justinian.[34] The

[32] The playwright attacks the French a second time later in the play,
when he has the "King of the Franks" welcome Antichrist, who states
that the "subtle wit" of the French has helped pave the way for him
(line 223). Michaelis (82) suggests that this is an attack on the theological
speculations of St. Bernard's enemy Peter Abelard.

[33] So far as I have been able to determine, none of the commentators
on the *Play of Antichrist* has suggested any connection between the play
and the revival of Roman law. For the suggestion that led to this
line of investigation I am indebted to the Rev. T. P. McLaughlin of the
Pontifical Institute of Mediaeval Studies.

[34] The standard work on the subject of Roman law in the Middle
Ages is F. K. von Savigny, *Geschichte des römischen Rechts im Mittelalter*
7 vols. (Heidelberg, 1834-51²), with an abbreviated French translation in
four volumes by C. Guenoux (Paris, 1839). For briefer discussions see
H. D. Hazeltine, "Roman and Canon Law in the Middle Ages," *Cambridge
Medieval History* 5 (Cambridge, 1926) 697-764; Émile Chénon, *Histoire*

Corpus was divided into four parts: the *Code* (imperial constitutions from the time of Hadrian down to Justinian), the *Digest* (a summary of earlier jurists' writings), the *Institutes* (a textbook for law students), and the *Novels* (Justinian's later legislation). The *Corpus*, and especially the *Digest*, present a body of law clearly and rationally written and arranged, particularly the laws dealing with the widespread commerce and navigation of classical times.[35] Roman law never died out completely after the fall of the Empire: the new barbarian rulers recognised the theory of the personality of the law, according to which each man inherited the law under which his father had lived, no matter where he made his home.[36] (This system was essential to the invaders because of their nomadic life.) Thus, while the new rulers lived under the Germanic common law, the former subjects of Rome continued to live under Roman law. But the subsistence economy and widespread illiteracy of the Dark Ages led to the abandonment of many of the complexities of the old Roman law, so that after a few centuries it came to be extremely simplified and debased. However, its customary use in the Midi and northern Italy, together with the fact that the Canon Law of the Church owed much to its language and techniques, kept it alive.

This was the situation in the north of Italy when Justinian's *Digest* was suddenly rediscovered about the year 1075.[37] A

générale du droit français public et privé des origines à 1815 (Paris, 1926) 1. 502-513; H. O. Taylor, *The Classical Heritage of the Middle Ages* (New York, 1957⁴) 56-70; and C. H. Haskins, *The Renaissance of the Twelfth Century* (New York, 1959²) 193-223.

[35] The essential difference between Roman law and the Common Law used throughout the English-speaking world lies not so much in the individual statutes of the two systems (though of course there are differences here) as in the method of arriving at them. Roman law is basically deductive: it begins with a set of principles and applies them to individual cases. Common law is inductive: it begins with immemorial custom and a series of individual case decisions and works up from there to principles — principles which are consequently often difficult to define.

[36] Hazeltine 728; Ewart Lewis, *Medieval Political Ideas* (New York, 1954) 2. 433.

[37] Chénon 504. See Paul Fournier, "Un tournant de l'histoire du droit: 1060-1140," *Nouvelle revue historique de droit français et étranger* 3 Ser. 40

fantastic story was later told about how it had been rescued from the flames of a burning building in Amalfi by some Pisans; this is clearly a myth, but it is a fact that the *Digest* had been hanging by a palaeographical thread. Because of the well known mediaeval respect for any written, certified authority, and because of the Italian cities' need for a more sophisticated body of legislation to govern their increasingly complex commercial enterprises, the rediscovered *Digest* was eagerly welcomed. The Law School at Bologna, under the great scholar Irnerius (called by his students the "lantern of the law"[38]), became the most important center for the study of the new law. Around Irnerius gathered what became known as the "school of Glossators" — scholars who added short notes called "glosses," first primarily verbal, then more technical in nature, to their copies of the *Digest* and other parts of the *Corpus*. These glosses soon came to equal the *Corpus* itself in bulk and reputation.

Irnerius's successors, Bulgar, Martin Gosia, Jacob, and Hugo of Ravenna, were known as the "four doctors." Their work, and the law which they were expounding, interested Frederick Barbarossa intensely — not for the practical reasons of commerce which attracted the Italian merchants, but because the *Corpus*, codified as it had been under the Emperor Justinian, appeared to give solid support to Frederick's dream of absolute sovereignty over his Empire — and perhaps over the whole Christian world.[39] The doctors confirmed the dictum of the *Digest* that "whatever pleases the prince has the force of law";[40] when Martin Gosia,

---

(1917) 129-180, for the developments that made the legal renaissance of the twelfth and thirteenth centuries possible.

[38] Chénon 505.

[39] For discussions of the concept of a universal empire see Lewis 2, 430-505 (who gives a number of selections of mediaeval works on law and political philosophy, all of which, however, are later than the twelfth century); J. B. Morrall, *Political Thought in Medieval Times* (London, 1960²) 81-103; R. W. and A. J. Carlyle, *A History of Mediaeval Political Theory in the West* 3 (Edinburgh and London, 1915) 170-180; the later weakening of the idea of universality is traced by Walter Ullmann, "The Development of the Medieval Idea of Sovereignty," *English Historical Review* 64 (1949) 1-33.

[40] *Gesta* 4.5; Chénon 507.

in response to a question from the Emperor, stated that he was indeed the "lord of the world" (*dominus mundi*), he was rewarded with Frederick's own palfrey. In 1158, the four doctors served as Frederick's legal advisors at the Diet which he called at Roncaglia to settle the legal position of the north Italian cities; they were probably responsible for the fact that the speeches he made and the laws he promulgated there were permeated with the influence of Roman law.[41]

The kings of France reacted with consternation to the rediscovered Roman law. Their reaction was based partly on the fear, which later turned out to be groundless, that the new law would be a threat to their domestic royal authority, which up to this time had been based solely on feudal custom.[42] Far more real was their fear of the support the law appeared to provide for the Emperor's claims to universal sovereignty. In retrospect, it is clear that these claims could never have been a *de facto* threat to French independence: even the control of Germany and Italy proved to be too taxing a job for the emperors' power. But in the twelfth century there could be no way of foreseeing this, and furthermore questions of *de jure* rights were taken very seriously in such a legalistic age.

The Church had proclaimed its opposition to the study of Roman law as early as the Council of Clermont (1130); the stated grounds were that its popularity threatened the primacy of the study of theology.[43] We can perhaps see the hand of the King of France in the restatement of this opposition by the Council of Tours (1163), the same council in which Louis and Henry refused to recognise Barbarossa's Pope Victor. Eventually King Philip Augustus asked Pope Honorius III to forbid the study of Roman law at the University of Paris, which was under the popes' jurisdiction. The result was the decretal *Super*

[41] In spite of this influence, however, most of the actual rights Frederick demanded at Roncaglia were not of Roman but of early Germanic origin. See Georges Blondel, "Étude sur les droits régaliens et la constitution de Roncaglia," *Mélanges Paul Fabre* (Paris, 1902) 236-257.

[42] Chénon 507.

[43] *Ibid.* 506.

speculam of 1219, which forbade its study on the grounds that "in the Ile-de-France and certain provinces men do not use the laws of the Roman emperors." [44]

The situation as it stood in 1160 is reflected in the *Play of Antichrist* by the previously mentioned claim of the Emperor of the Romans that "the writings of historians" prove that the whole world had been granted to the Roman emperor as a "fief." The only Christian king who opposes this claim is the "King of the Franks." He maintains that once his ancestors, the "Gauls" (by whom he presumably means Charlemagne) possessed the Empire, and that rightfully it therefore belongs to him. He thus ignores the claim of Roman law, as did his historical counterpart, and states in opposition his claim that Charlemagne, the earlier possessor of the Empire, was a Frenchman. This claim about Charlemagne was actually used by the French jurists, and in just such a way as in this play: not as a serious claim to leadership of the Holy Roman Empire, but as a counterclaim to the universal pretentions of the German emperors. [45]

The opposition of the French king is ended by force in the *Play of Antichrist*, but historically the solution was much less precipitous. Both the King of France and the Emperor were being challenged by overly powerful vassals: for France, there was Henry II of England; for the Emperor, Henry the Lion of Saxony. In the face of this opposition the two monarchs drew

----

[44] "Quia tamen in Francia et nonnullis provinciis romanorum imperatorum legibus non utantur," quoted *ibid.* 508. The text of the decretal is given in Marcel Fournier, "L'Église et le droit romain au XIIIᵉ siècle: à propos de l'interprétation de la bulle *Super speculam* d'Honorius III, qui interdit l'enseignement du droit romain à Paris," *Nouvelle revue historique de droit français et étranger* 3 Ser. 14 (1890) 115-118. For discussions see Lewis 2, 434; Alfred de Curzon, "L'enseignement du droit français dans les universités de France aux XVIIᵉ et XVIIIᵉ siècles," *Nouvelle revue historique de droit français et étranger* 3 Ser. 43 (1919) 214-215; and Paul Fournier, "Inauguration d'une chaire d'histoire du droit canonique à la Faculté de droit de l'Université de Paris," *Revue historique de droit français et étranger* 4 Ser. 1 (1922) 250. Marcel Fournier's article (105-109) gives arguments against the generally accepted theory that this decretal was proclaimed at the request of Philip Augustus.

[45] Lewis 2, 433; Gaines Post, "Two Notes on Nationalism in the Middle Ages: II. Rex Imperator," *Traditio* 9 (1953) 315.

closer together, and by 1187 Frederick and the French king (now Philip Augustus) had formed a firm alliance.[46] The *de facto* question of imperial universality was thus solved: it would become a dead letter completely in the next century with the rapid weakening of the Empire. Meanwhile the jurists in the law schools of northern Italy were working on the *de jure* problem.[47] These scholars were an international group, and seem to have had a close grip on reality as well as the interests of their own nations. By the end of the twelfth century and the beginning of the thirteenth, jurists like Richard de Mores of England and the Spaniard Vincentius were working out the formula which solved the problem of the imperial claims: *rex est imperator in regno suo* ("the king is emperor in his own realm"). With the burden of the claim of imperial universality thus removed, the Roman law was free to be used in strengthening the position of the royal autocracies which became the nations of modern Europe.

After the submission of the King of the Franks in the play, the Emperor next challenges the "King of the Greeks," who represents the Byzantine *Basileus*. This challenge perhaps mirrors the conflict between Frederick and the *Basileus* over rights in Sicily and southern Italy.[48] The surrender of the "King of the Greeks" is not wholly fanciful; although Byzantium was still an empire of incomparable material splendor, its actual power relative to the West was rapidly shrinking during the twelfth century. At the beginning of the thirteenth, Constantinople fell to the armies of the Fourth Crusade.

The climax of the reign of the Emperor of the Romans in the *Play of Antichrist* — his rescue of Jerusalem, his war with the "King of Babylonia," and his surrender of the imperial crown — shows a thorough mixture of legend and history. The *Pseudo-Methodius* and the *Tiburtina* had told of the Last Emperor's

---

[46] Poole 397.

[47] Brian Tierney, "Some Recent Works on the Political Theories of the Medieval Canonists 2: Regnum et Imperium," *Traditio* 10 (1954) 612-619; Post 296-320; de Curzon 215.

[48] Poole 396.

victorious battle with the infidels from the East.[49] But the true
history of the First and Second Crusades, both of which had
taken place within the memory of living men at the time the
play was written, invested this legend with a new reality in the
eyes of the *Antichrist* playwright. The Christian King of
Jerusalem who calls for help, and the gathering of all the
Christian kings of Europe to answer this call, are both vivid
reflections of true history which the playwright added to his
legendary material. He of course had no way of knowing that
within thirty years this part of the play would be re-enacted in
reality with disastrous results both for his hero Frederick and
for western Christendom.

With the abdication of the Roman Emperor and the advent of
Antichrist, the play enters the realm of eschatology, where, as
we might expect, actual contemporary history plays a minimal
role. One more facet of imperial propaganda, however, was re-
tained for exposure at this point. By reducing the pope to a minor
character called "Apostolicus" who sits in silence throughout the
play,[50] even when the crusade to liberate Jerusalem is called
(here the play is blatantly unhistorical, for the summoning of
crusades had always been the pope's prerogative), the *Antichrist*
playwright had already made his position in the controversy
between Frederick and the popes clear. Now, with the approach
of Antichrist, he turned his weapons on the reformers who were
adherents of the papal party in contemporary Germany. He
introduced into his play[51] the "Hypocrites," who go about

[49] See the preceding section of this introduction, which deals with the
legendary background of the play.
[50] This is the explanation most commentators offer for the minor role
the pope has in the play (see Young 2, 393; Chambers 2, 64). But
Michaelis (82-83) defends the role of the pope, pointing out that he is
the only character never to fall to Antichrist's blandishments, while
Wilhelm Meyer, *Gesammelte Abhandlungen zur mittellateinischen Rythmik*
(Berlin, 1905) 1, 146, states quite rightly that the legendary material the
playwright used provided no role for the pope. Langosch (92) also denies
that the playwright is attacking the pope. Wilhelm Creisenach, *Geschichte
des neueren Dramas* 1 (Halle, 1893) 85n, offers the tentative suggestion
that Antichrist is to be identified with Pope Alexander III.
[51] Wilhelm Scherer, "Zum Tergenseer Antichristspiel," *Zeitschrift für
deutsches Altertum* 24 (1880) 455, suggests that the Hypocrites are to be

consciously paving the way for Antichrist by corrupting good
Christians and denouncing "worldly priests" — i.e., the secular
clergy who supported the Emperor against the Pope. Proof that
this satirical attack hit home (and one of the major evidences
for dating the *Play of Antichrist* in 1160) is found in a treatise,
De investigatione Antichristi, written in 1161 by the reformer
Gerhoh of Reichersberg, a supporter of the papal party.[52] In
this sermon on evil Gerhoh attacks clerics who present plays on
such subjects as Antichrist and the Nativity in churches; "the
general argument of the chapter in which this passage occurs is
that the clergy who promote plays within the churches are
carrying out the work of that very Antichrist whom they
represent upon the stage."[53] It is quite possible that this attack
is a reaction to the very play we possess.

The account presented above has, I hope, made it clear that
the *Play of Antichrist* is in large measure a political tract, the
product of a man who was vitally interested in the important
controversies of his day. It should be equally clear, however,
that the play is not "historical" even in the sense that the freely
written history plays of Shakespeare are. In spite of its many
historical reflections the play deals more with the legendary
future than with the past or present. But the modern reader
should remember that to the mediaeval mind the future End of
the World was a real part of "history" in the larger sense. (For
example, Frederick Barbarossa's uncle and biographer, Otto of
Freising, included an account of the End of the World in his
universal history, *The Two Cities*.[54]) Indeed, the predictions in

identified with the Hospitalers, Templars, and Syrian barons, whose
coöperation with Islam was so disillusioning to the newly arrived
Crusaders.

[52] See Chambers 2, 64, 98-99; Young 2, 392-393. The text of the
chapter of *De investigatione Antichristi* in which Gerhoh denounces drama
("De spectaculis theatricis in ecclesia Dei exhibitis") is printed in Young
2, 524-525.

[53] Young 2, 393.

[54] Otto of Freising, *The Two Cities*, tr. C. C. Mierow (Columbia
University Records of Civilization [9], New York, 1928) 453-514. Emil
Michael, *Geschichte des deutschen Volkes vom dreizehnten Jahrhundert bis zum
Ausgang des Mittelalters* 4 (Freiburg, 1906) 434, suggests the possibility that
this part of Otto's work was the major source for the *Play of Antichrist*.

the *Play of Antichrist* are presented broadly enough and are
based upon a close enough view of reality to be surprisingly
accurate. Frederick Barbarossa did in fact lead a crusade to
free the Holy Land from the Moslem threat in 1187, and as part
of this crusade he sent messengers to the *Basileus* of Byzantium
demanding, if not recognition of his sovereignty, at least certain
privileges for his crusaders. But with his accidental death by
drowning in a stream in Cilicia the parallel with the play fails.
The death of Barbarossa marked the practical end both of the
crusading spirit and the hopes for a universal Roman Empire
which are celebrated in the *Play of Antichrist*.[55]

[55] Appropriately enough, after his death Frederick soon joined the
ranks of those emperors whose return was predicted in folklore, thus
becoming a true candidate for the title of Last Roman Emperor (Bryce,
177-178). In the thirteenth century St. Thomas Aquinas reconciled the
growing weakness of the Empire with the failure of Antichrist to appear
by suggesting that the "power" which 2 Thess. 2.6 said was holding
Antichrist in check was the Church rather than the Empire (Lewis 2,
619).

CHARACTERISATION AND STRUCTURE

Characterisation in the *Play of Antichrist* is rudimentary and monumental. There is no differentiation of individuals through speech: as far as style is concerned, any speech could be assigned to any character. There is little individualisation through action: in general, characters march through their roles like the majestic but indistinguishable figures on a Byzantine mosaic. To a certain extent the King of the Franks is an exception: he responds to the Emperor's demand for homage with an outburst of self-confidence, but abases himself most humbly, and with no sign of resentment, as soon as he is defeated. Despite his earlier bravado, he falls to Antichrist with no resistance whatever, and in the basest way possible: in response to Antichrist's bribery. But all this cannot be called true "characterisation": in his bravado, cowardice, and greed, the Frankish king is simply a representative of the dramatic type of the *miles gloriosus* (the "braggart warrior") — and a rather pale representative at that, for he lacks the comic exaggeration that the type exhibits in Plautus and later playwrights.[1] The Emperor of the Romans, with his steadfastness, strength, and self-confidence, is largely a stereotyped but monumental representation of the Noble King. His cautious attitude toward Antichrist's blandishments, however, does individualise him slightly. The other kings are marked out by no special traits. In the figure of Antichrist we might have imagined that there were great possibilities for dramatic characterisation; however, even in the plain and brief narrative of the Gospels (Matt. 4.1-11), Satan is far more of an individual than is the Antichrist of this play. Rather than exhibiting the subtlety, eloquence, and sophistic intelligence we should expect to find in

---

[1] By this I do not mean to imply that Plautus's comedies had any influence on the *Play of Antichrist*; on the contrary, if its author had read Plautus's work carefully enough to have learned anything from it (and it is in fact unlikely that he had ever heard of Plautus), he would have written a very different play. I am simply using *miles gloriosus* as a handy tag for a stock dramatic figure.

the role, Antichrist simply follows the Rules for the Behaviour
of Antichrist laid down in Adso's *Essay*: he uses gifts, threats,
force, and false miracles to seduce the faithful; he terrorises
unbelievers and demands the homage of all mankind. The Jews,
also, are not individualised, but simply do whatever is expected
of them at any given moment of the plot (though this in itself,
as we shall see later, represents a considerable achievement on
the part of a mediaeval playwright). As for the Prophets,
Enoch and Elijah, an indication of the quality of characterisation allowed to them is found in the fact that their longest
speech is little more than a versified conflation of the Athanasian
and Apostles' Creeds (see notes to lines 329-350 of the play).
The Emperor's messengers and Antichrist's servants, the Hypocrites, are virtually indistinguishable, while Ecclesia (the Church),
Synagoga (Jewry), and Gentilitas (the Heathen) are mouthpieces
for dogmatic chants.

But, although skill in characterisation can make a good play,
lack of it does not necessarily ruin one. Some of the greatest and
deepest of the Greek tragedies, such as Aeschylus's *Seven against
Thebes*, are almost totally devoid of characterisation, and true
individualisation in any sort of narrative is generally speaking a
very recent development in the history of western literature, even
though we, in the age of the Novel, are liable to regard it as the
touchstone of literary excellence.[2] Critics have learned to look
beyond characterisation, notably to poetic quality and to structure
and plot, in judging a literary work.

The verse of the play is technically competent, surprisingly so
when we consider its early position in the history of mediaeval
Latin rhymed poetry, and it displays a considerable amount of
the impressive sonority, the "power," that Otto of Freising,
fellow-countryman and contemporary of our playwright, re-

[2] Contemporary critics, particularly in the field of drama, are making
a conscious effort to turn away from this attitude; see, for example,
G. Wilson Knight's work on Shakespeare. But a full realisation of how
unimportant individual characterisation was to earlier authors is still very
difficult for a modern reader. The best study of the problem of realism
and characterisation in the history of western literature is Erich Auerbach's brilliant *Mimesis: The Representation of Reality in Western Literature*,
tr. Willard Trask (Princeton, 1953; Anchor Books 1957).

cognised as the hallmark of the Latin language.[3] There is also
a high degree of technical virtuosity in the playwright's manipu-
lation of changing rhythmical schemes (see below for a fuller
discussion of the rhythm and versification of the play). But we
cannot claim for this verse any of the lyrical beauty or flashing
insight that is the essence of real poetry. It is to plot and
structure, rather than poetry, that we must turn if we are to find
any special literary value in this play.

Although the plot of the *Play of Antichrist* is simple, it has
a complication which would appear at the outset to leave it open
to a serious charge of lack of unity. The play seems to fall into
two entirely separate and independent parts. In the first half,
the Roman Emperor acquires dominion over the whole world
and after his triumph resigns his crown and royal dignity to God
and the Church. The second half consists of the advent and
temporary triumph of Antichrist, followed by his final defeat at
the hands of God; the Emperor seems completely forgotten. This
apparent disunity has led some editors and commentators to
suggest that instead of the *Play of Antichrist*, the work ought to
be called the *Play of the Roman Emperor and of Antichrist.*[4]
But as a matter of fact the disunity exists only on the surface;
far from being separate and distinct, the two parts of the play
are formed, thanks to the talents of the playwright, into a close-
knit and complementary whole.

As I have indicated earlier in this introduction, the prophecy
of the Last Roman Emperor had by the twelfth century become
an indispensable part of the eschatology of Antichrist. Since
mediaeval interest in this eschatology was so wide-spread, and
since we can safely assume that the audience of any mediaeval
Latin play must have been literate and educated, we could easily
at this point fall back upon the explanation (unfortunately so

3 Otto of Freising, *The Two Cities*, tr. C. C. Mierow (Columbia University Records of Civilization [9], New York, 1928) 1, 27 (quoted in
Mierow's Introduction, p. 40).

4 For example, Karl Langosch, who calls his translation of the play
"Das Spiel vom deutschen Kaiser und vom Antichrist" in his *Geistliche
Spiele* (Berlin, 1957[2]) 179. (No title for the play is found in the MS, but
most scholars call it *Ludus de Antichristo*.)

prevalent in criticism of Greek tragedy[5]) of the audience's
previous knowledge of the plot of the play. Thus we could
excuse the apparent lack of connection between the two halves
of the play by suggesting that what the playwright had in-
competently left out of his play the audience with its foreknow-
ledge could fill in. This excuse, however, is not necessary. Even
if we did not know that historically the Last Roman Emperor
was part and parcel of the Antichrist legend, the author of the
Play of Antichrist has shown us by his skilful dramatic technique
that he considers the two stories to be a unity illustrating the
same basic truth, the inability of man to defeat evil without the
help of God.

The Emperor of the Romans accomplishes all that human
power, unaided by direct divine intervention, can do. With all
the appurtenances of human strength — law, custom, military
power, and force of character — on his side, he gains control
over all that human might and glory have to offer. He then
gives it all to God — a gift that consists, in short, of the
totality of human accomplishment. But as he makes this gift to
God, he addresses Him as

> ... Thee ...
> Through Whom kings reign, and Whom alone we call
> The Emperor and Ruler of us all.   (lines 148-150)

The way is now open for this truth, that God is He "through
Whom kings reign," to be demonstrated by the advent of Antichrist. The Emperor has used all the strengths of humanity to
reach the highest peak humanity is capable of ascending. Antichrist now proceeds to use all the weaknesses of humanity to
demonstrate the ephemerality of humanity's achievement and to
destroy it. Through human greed, cowardice, weakness, and
credulity, the Emperor's human accomplishments collapse one by
one. Between the Emperor's ascendancy and that of Antichrist
the parallels, both in words and action, are clearly enough drawn
to be immediately recognisable in the fast-moving world of the

---

[5] For an excellent answer to this theory, based mainly on a comparison
between the dramatic exposition in the Greek tragedians with the lack
of it in Seneca, see N. T. Pratt, *Dramatic Suspense in Seneca and in his
Greek Precursors* (Princeton, 1939).

theater, yet subtly enough to avoid the charge of obvious preaching. Like the Emperor, Antichrist sends his messengers to all the kings of the world one by one announcing the advent of a new power which must be obeyed. As with the Emperor, these kings submit after some display of obviously futile resistance. The words Antichrist uses to welcome them into his fold are almost identical with those the Emperor used to accept the fealty of his vassal kings.[6] In both cases, Gentilitas (Heathendom) is the last to fall: after singing a defiant hymn praising polytheism, she is defeated by force of arms, first the Emperor's, then Antichrist's. Now that Antichrist has conquered Gentilitas, evil is triumphant over the world of men. Human goodness, even when it possesses divine truth, can do nothing to change this world. This is illustrated by the fate of the Jews, who up to this point in the play have been silent. After falling to Antichrist (a fall which, significantly, breaks the parallel between Antichrist's career and the Emperor's), the Jews are immediately redeemed by the message of the Prophets, Enoch and Elijah. But their acceptance of this message has no effect on a world over which evil has triumphed. All that the Prophets and the Jews can do is suffer martyrdom to bear witness to the truth. Here the reader must imagine the stage setting, as the kings of the earth, totally seduced by evil, watch impassively from their platforms in all their pomp and glory as the only bearers of truth to be found in the world are destroyed by evil — a striking contrast to the conclusion of the Emperor's reign, when the kings gathered in magnificent array, complete with a chorus and an angel singing from Heaven, to rescue the beseiged Holy City of Jerusalem. Now only the lone voice of Ecclesia is heard, as she sings in quiet and loving recognition of the glorious martyrdom of the Prophets and the Jews:

A bundle of myrrh is my well-beloved unto me.

Human strength, even armed with truth, is clearly helpless. The only thing that can save the temporal world of humanity from the results of human weakness and evil is the direct intervention

6 Compare, for example, lines 217-218, where Antichrist welcomes the King of the Greeks, with 93-94, spoken by the Emperor to the King of the Franks.

of God. And this is exactly what concludes the play: Antichrist summons all the world to worship him, and just when he is saying, "peace and safety," he is destroyed by a thunderbolt from Heaven, and mankind, forgiven, returns to God.

A critic might object that the conclusion of the *Play of Antichrist* seems very abrupt and brief. Including the stage directions, it runs as follows in the MS:

> Suddenly there is a crash of thunder over the head of Antichrist, and, as he and all his men flee, Ecclesia sings:
>
> > Lo, this is the man who made not God his strength.
> > But I am like a green olive tree in the house of God.
>
> Then, as everyone returns to the faith, Ecclesia, welcoming them, begins:
>
> > Praise our God.

To answer this objection, we should first take our cue from the word "begins" in the second stage direction. The very least this implies is that "Praise our God" (quoted from Apoc. 19.5) is not all that Ecclesia sings at the end of the play. We are therefore justified in expanding "Praise our God" somewhat, drawing on its Biblical context for this expansion; the result is

> Praise our God, all ye His servants,
> And ye that fear Him, both small and great.

This is the least that "begins" allows, and I have expanded my own translation thus. But if we may use only a little imagination, it will be clear that this point in the play is an obvious place for some sort of responsory, such as that found at line 146a, when the seige of Jerusalem is lifted. Such a responsory might run as follows (for my text I draw again on the relevant parts of the Biblical quotation):

Ecclesia: Praise our God, all ye His servants,
          And ye that fear Him, both small and great.

    All: Alleluia, for the Lord God omnipotent reigneth.
          Let us be glad and rejoice, and give honour to Him:
          For the marriage of the Lamb is come,
          And his wife hath made herself ready.
          Praise our God, all ye His servants,
          And ye that fear Him, both small and great.

This, of course, is pure conjecture, and I offer it as such here only, and not in my text. But it is hard to imagine the play without some such conclusion, if only for the practical theatrical reason of providing a recessional to clear the stage of its enormous cast.

Even if this expansion is granted, however, a critic might go on to object that the play still might have been improved by the addition of some sort of denouement, to give the characters a chance to reflect upon the depths of their delusion and the enormity of their sin. But such an objection would betray a lack of understanding of the *Antichrist* playwright's basic purpose and a substitution for it of a characteristically modern interest in psychology. The playwright is interested only in the graphic depiction of the enormous power of evil; unlike a modern writer, he simply takes for granted a natural weakness in men that will lead then to fall to this evil unless aided by God.[7] Therefore an examination of the mental processes of his characters would for him be beside the point. A brief examination of two tragedies by Euripides,[8] both of which, like our play, end in divine intervention, might make the position of the *Antichrist* playwright clearer. When Hippolytus, in the play of the same name, is dragged onto the stage crushed and dying as the result of the curse of his father, Theseus, the goddess Artemis appears and exposes to Theseus and Hippolytus the sins ("errors" would perhaps be a better word, since the Greeks did not share the Christian concept of "sin") they have committed. Rather than simply end the play here, Euripides allows

[7] Here he differs from his predecessor St. Augustine, who in his *Confessions* devoted a great deal of psychologically oriented thought to the question of what in man makes him fall to evil. This difference between Augustine and the *Antichrist* playwright is a clear example of the fact that literary history does not run a clear and continuous path of "progress"; the *Play of Antichrist* is closer in spirit to Aeschylus than to Augustine.

[8] I hope the reader will realise that what follows is only a brief discussion of a small facet in two complex plays. The best modern translations of these plays are to be found in David Grene and Richmond Lattimore, edd., *The Complete Greek Tragedies* (Chicago, 1959) *Hippolytus*: 3, 157-221; *Orestes*: 4, 185-288.

his characters a considerable number of lines to discuss and mourn their fates. In this dialogue it becomes clear that while Theseus has gained a certain measure of self-knowledge from his tragedy, Hippolytus has learned nothing from his. Thus the denouement makes it clear that there is something in the character of a totally one-sided man (Hippolytus, in this case) that makes it impossible for him to learn anything from experience. But in Euripides's *Orestes*, a play which has been called "tragedy utterly without affirmation, an image of heroic action seen as botched, disfigured, and sick, carried along by the machinery and slogans of heroic action in a steady crescendo of biting irony and the rage of exposure,"[9] when the train of unremitting evil is suddenly and ironically cut off by the intervention of Apollo *ex machina*, the characters simply walk off the stage with hardly a word. This is because Euripides in this play is interested only in presenting as vivid a picture as possible of total human depravity — in this case the depravity he found in the ancient heroic myth of the revenge of Orestes. Any examination of conscience on the part of the characters would only serve to weaken the intensity of this picture: hence the absence of any real denouement to the play.

The *Play of Antichrist* is similar to the *Orestes* rather than the *Hippolytus*, except that our playwright is demonstrating the extent of human weakness rather than human depravity. When this point has been made, all that remains is to restore order and clear the stage with as much dignity as possible. This is done by means of the songs quoted above (whatever their full extent might have been) and by a symbolic procession of the entire cast. Note the stage direction quoted above: "as everyone returns to the faith." The cast has previously (line 408) gathered around the platform representing the Temple to worship Antichrist. Now, singing the praises of God, they proceed to Rome, the "seat of the Pope and the Church," and the play is over.

---

[9] Quoted from William Arrowsmith's introduction to the *Orestes, The Complete Greek Tragedies* 4, 186.

RHYTHM AND MUSIC

The use of verbal sound effects in the *Play of Antichrist* is strikingly original and deserves discussion even in an introduction to a translation of the play.[1] Rhythm and music are used throughout to embellish and reinforce the play's structure. At the opening of the play, the allegorical representatives of what to the playwright were the two major non-Christian religions of the world, Judaism and Heathendom, both sing "credos" which are rhymed, stanzaic songs with a form reminiscent of Christian hymns.[2] Ecclesia (the Church) also enters to musical accompaniment, this time the processional chant *Alto consilio*,[3] with a refrain written especially for the play. Most of the body of the play is written in rhymed couplets of thirteen syllables; for example, lines 55-56:

> *Reges ergo singuli   prius instituta*
> *Nunc Romano solvant   inperio tributa.*

The constraining influence of the rhyme, which, as in most Latin rhymed verse of the High Middle Ages, is "feminine," tends to make the lines rather wooden; this effect is broken up, however, by the constant shifting of the main caesura, which sometimes falls after the sixth syllable (e.g., line 49: *Sicut scripta tradunt / hystoriographorum*), sometimes after the seventh syllable (line 50: *Totus mundus fuerat / fiscus Romanorum*), and occasionally does not appear at all (line 51: *Hoc primorum strenuitas elaboravit*).

---

[1] The metrics of the play are discussed in full by Wilhelm Meyer, *Gesammelte Abhandlungen zur mittellateinischen Rythmik* (Berlin, 1905) 1, 334-338.

[2] For the rhythmical structure of the most important mediaeval Latin hymns, see F. A. March, *Latin Hymns* (New York, 1891) 319-328.

[3] "No appropriate hymn or trope beginning *Alto consilio* has been found," but the technical term *conductus* in the stage directions clearly indicates that a processional chant was used in this part of the play: Karl Young, *The Drama of the Medieval Church* (Oxford, 1933, 1962²) 2, 373.

A number of high points in the play have been underscored by
a change in meter.[4] When the Emperor of the Romans is
gathering the army that will liberate Jerusalem from the King
of Babylonia, a chorus sings the responsory *Iudea et Ierusalem*,
written in the cantillation style familiar from Gregorian chant
(line 140a). When Antichrist announces his arrival and gives his
first instructions to Hypocrisy and Heresy, he uses short lines,
alternating between couplets with eight syllables in each line
(line 151: *mei regni venit hora*) and couplets with eleven syllables
per line (line 153: *fiat, ut conscendam regni solium*). He afterwards reverts to the play's normal rhythmical pattern. When
Antichrist's men drive the King of Jerusalem from his throne,
they sing a line from Psalm 88 (KJV 89) in cantillation style
(line 186a). The Prophets, Enoch and Elijah, use an eleven-
syllable line, even while those characters with whom they are
conversing continue to use the normal thirteen-syllable line; this
technique effectively sets these visitors from Heaven apart from
the rest of the characters of the play. While they and the Jews
are being martyred by Antichrist's servants, Ecclesia sings the
beautiful line from the Song of Songs, "A bundle of myrrh is my
well-beloved unto me," once again in the style of Gregorian
chant (line 401). Finally, at the close of the play, Ecclesia sings
equally impressive lines from the Psalms and the Apocalypse in
a similar style.

In an uninflected language like English any attempt to
reproduce fully all these various rhythms would do great violence
to the literal meaning of the text.[5] On the other hand, a prose
translation would give an equally wrong impression: the play's
rhyme and rhythm add immeasurably to its stateliness and
formality. I have compromised by using for most of the play

[4] Another example of the play's originality. The use of a referential
metrical system in poetry is far rarer than is often thought. Scholars
claim to find the phenomenon in classical Latin poetry (see C. G.
Cooper, *An Introduction to the Latin Hexameter* (Melbourne, 1952) 20-48),
but none of their examples are so convincing as those in this play.

[5] In German, however, Karl Langosch has done an impressive job in
translating the entire play with its original rhythm and rhyme scheme in
Geistliche Spiele (Berlin, 1957²) 179-239.

a line that is basically blank verse, with rhyme at the end of each speech. Where shorter lines are used, as in the speeches of Antichrist and the Prophets, I have shortened my own lines and used more rhyme. The lines in cantillation style are given as prose.

The extent to which music was used in the play is uncertain. The only place where musical notation actually appears is with the first three words of the responsory *Iudea et Ierusalem* (line 146a).[6] On the other hand, most of the speeches are introduced in the stage directions with *cantat, cantant, cantans*, etc.; this might be taken to indicate that all of the lines of the play were sung, except for two facts: first, the metaphorical use of "singing" for any kind of poetry including spoken verse was more than a thousand years old when this play was written, and second, in ten different instances, none of which appear to be any different from the rest of the play, the stage directions use the word "saying" to introduce a speech.[7]

My conjecture, which I have no way of proving, would be that the stanzaic songs of Gentilitas and Synagoga were sung, as their form would indicate, like hymns, thus balancing the entrance of Ecclesia, which is accompanied by a processional chant. The four examples of rhythmical prose noted above were perhaps done in a manner similar to Gregorian chant. The remainder of the play was probably declaimed in a formal manner.

I should add that for purposes of aesthetic analysis an unassailable answer to this question is not necessary. What is important is that at various high points of the play, sound and rhythm instantly recognisable as different from that of the rest of the play were employed. Sound, however exploited, supported the play's dramatic structure.

6 Young 2, 376n.

7 *Dicentes* is used before the speech beginning at line 229, *dicens* before lines 219, 261, 275, 279, 285, 298a (a duplicate of the speech which begins at line 215 and is introduced by *cantat*), 325, 361, and 395. Such alternation of directive supports the theory that the actors were expected to declaim their lines.

STAGING

Although the stage directions for the *Play of Antichrist* are fuller than those of most mediaeval Latin plays, they still present a number of difficult problems. Where was the play produced — in a church, in a public square, or elsewhere? What exactly were the *sedes* (lit. "seats") on which the players stood (or sat)? And how were these *sedes* arranged?

The rubrics[1] give no direct evidence as to where the play was produced. But since the mediaeval Latin drama is descended from the liturgy, and since it is definitely clear that most of these dramas were produced in churches, and since there were very few other places where a mediaeval play could be produced, we should expect *prima facie* that the *Play of Antichrist*, too, was staged in a church.[2] Most probably this would be a church connected with the monastery at Tegernsee; perhaps the playwright's fellow monks supplied the immense cast.[3] (This would be the most logical source for such a large number of players capable of singing in Latin.) It has also been suggested that the play was staged in a public square.[4] No positive answer to this

---

[1] "Rubric" is a liturgical term, which in this context means "stage direction."

[2] This suggestion is also strengthened by Gerhoh of Reichersberg's statement in his *De investigatione Antichristi* (in which he complains, among other things, about "so-called priests" presenting plays about Antichrist) that such players "have even reached the point of changing the very churches, houses of prayer, into theaters." Quoted by Karl Young, *The Drama of the Medieval Church* (Oxford, 1933, 1962²) 2, 392; my translation.

[3] Even if we assign only one actor to roles like "the messengers of the Emperor" and "the Hypocrites," the play still contains seventeen speaking roles and eleven mute roles. There could, furthermore, be very little doubling of roles, since almost all the characters are on the stage throughout the play. Most of the mediaeval Latin drama does not even approach the *Play of Antichrist* in size of cast.

[4] See Young 2, 394; the main reason for this suggestion is the play's large cast. It is also possible that the play was written for a command performance in the Emperor's court.

question is possible, but it would seem that the burden of proof lies with those who would maintain that the play was produced anywhere but in a church.

The opening rubric states that, in addition to the Temple at Jerusalem, the stage consists of "seven royal seats" (*vii sedes regales*). The term *sedes* is a broad one, covering anything from "chair" to "place." (We have similar metaphorical uses of the English word "seat.") The "seven seats" in the *Play of Antichrist* could not simply have been "seven chairs," since one of them, that of the Emperor of the Romans, is at one point occupied by the Emperor, his army, Ecclesia, the Pope, the Clergy, and presumably (although the rubric is silent on this point) by the allegorical figures of Justice and Mercy which accompany Ecclesia — all at the same time.[5] Yet at another point it is explicitly stated that the Emperor is seated while being addressed by the King of the Franks.[6] We can therefore conclude that the *sedes* were raised[7] platforms, representing nations or cities, each of which supported one or more thrones as the plot demanded.

The play's chief staging problem is the arrangement of these platforms. Directions for their arrangement are given in the first rubric, which includes two different expressions meaning "to the south." The platform of the King of the Greeks is to be placed *ad austrum*, that of the King of Babylonia and Gentilitas *ad meridiem*. Why should this distinction be made? It is possible that *ad austrum* is a textual error: the expression *ad aquilonem* ("to the north") might at some point in the history of the text have been abbreviated *ad ā*, and this abbreviation later incorrectly expanded.[8] Or perhaps the playwright was using *ad austrum* in some peculiar Germanic way, meaning "to the east

[5] See rubric following line 48.

[6] See rubric following line 85.

[7] It is clear from the rubrics that the platforms were raised; for example, in the rubric following line 32, "she [Gentilitas] and the King of Babylonia ascend their platform (*ascendunt in sedem suam*)." (Perhaps it is worth adding that Latin *ascendere* need not mean "to go up.")

[8] This is one suggestion made by Eduard Michaelis, "Zum Ludus de Antichristo," *Zeitschrift für deutsches Altertum* 54 (1913) 79.

(*osten*) of Germany," as is found in the Latin form *Austria* for the German *Österreich*.[9] This last interpretation has perhaps the advantage of placing Greece in a geographically more correct position. But even if we accept the use of two different expressions meaning "to the south,"[10] we are still left with the difficulty of determining how the platforms were to be arranged in a church. If the ordering of the rubric is followed, the north side of the playing area would be left open, presumably for the spectators. But if we assume, as I think we must, that our church would follow the almost universal pattern of being laid out on an east-west line, with the altar on the east end and the main entrance on the west, we should expect the *west* side of the playing area to be left open for the spectators. Thus the structure representing the Temple of the Lord would be set at the church's altar, and in fact the play makes explicit mention of an altar in the Temple.[11] An interesting attempt to solve these difficulties has been made by one commentator,[12] who suggests the following arrangement: The platforms are grouped in a semicircle, open to the spectators, who are on the west side facing east. On the far left end of this semicircle is the platform of the King of the Franks. Then comes the *imperium*,[13] the platform for the Emperor, Ecclesia, and the Pope. Next are the platforms of the King of the Teutons, the King of the Greeks, and the King of Jerusalem. In the center of the semicircle, furthest from the spectators, stands the Temple of the Lord. Then, as the semicircle swings back toward the spectators, come the platforms of Synagoga, the King of Babylonia and Gentilitas, and finally, closest to the spectators, the heathen idol.[14] This suggested

[9] Michaelis 80.

[10] Young (2, 388n.) says, a little ingenuously, that he sees "no serious obstacle to our accepting two different expressions meaning 'south'." Of course we must in the end accept the two expressions, but their use is nonetheless odd.

[11] See the rubric following line 146a. On this altar the Emperor of the Romans lays down his sceptre and crown.

[12] See Michaelis's diagram (80).

[13] This term is often used in the play for the Emperor's platform, e.g. in the rubric following line 114.

[14] This idol is not mentioned in the opening rubric; it appears in the

arrangement is attractive for a number of reasons. First, its symmetry: the Temple in the center of the semicircle neatly divides the world into two halves, Christians on the spectators' left and non-Christians on their right. Second, it simplifies production in the curved apse of a church, with the church's altar standing in the center of the arrangement, in the Temple. Third, it is geographically intelligible and suited to the world picture of mediaeval man, whose usual map of the world, unlike ours, was arranged with the east at the top.[15] In spite of these advantages, the arrangement has not been accepted by succeeding scholars, mainly because of the difficulties of reconciling it with the directions of the opening rubric.[16]

The rubrics make only a few remarks regarding the costuming of the players. Ecclesia is dressed in woman's garments, as are Mercy, who carries oil, and Justice, who carries scales and a sword.[17] Antichrist has a breastplate hidden under his garments.[18] The kings have crowns, which they offer to Antichrist on becoming his vassals. No mention is made of any special costume for the King of Babylonia or Gentilitas. Since a distinctive costume for Jews had not yet been universally imposed,[19] it is impossible to tell how these players were dressed. It is probable,

rubric following line 298, where it is struck down by the messenger of Antichrist.

[15] According to Michaelis (*ibid.*) the typical world map of this period had the shape of a circle; the top half of the circle was Asia, the bottom left fourth Europe, and the bottom right fourth Africa. His staging would place the heathen (i.e. Moslems) in Africa, but as he points out (81) Cairo was the seat of the Islamic Caliphate at this time.

[16] See Young 2, 388 and Karl Langosch, *Politische Dichtung um Kaiser Friedrich Barbarossa* (Berlin, 1943) 288. But as Michaelis (79) points out, there were at this time no national colors or anthems to distinguish different nations, and heraldry was still in its infancy; it is hard to see how the anarchic arrangement favored by Young and Langosch could have been understood by the audience.

[17] See rubric following line 44.

[18] See rubric following line 150.

[19] Such a universal decree was passed by the Fourth Lateran Council in 1215, Title 68; see Friedrich Heer, *The Medieval World*, tr. J. Sondheimer (London, 1962) 255 and Walter Ullmann, *Medieval Papalism* (London, 1949) 122 for explanations of it.

however, that the actor playing Synagoga wore a blindfold.[20]
Bearing in mind the mediaeval love and talent for pomp and
pageantry, we can be quite certain that the costumes of all the
characters were brilliantly colorful and impressively dignified.[21]

[20] See note 72 of the play.

[21] A medieval drawing showing Antichrist giving presents to the kings
of the world is reproduced in Young (facing 2, 388); although there is
no evidence that this drawing is connected with the *Play of Antichrist,*
it suggests the kind of costuming that might have been used in a
production of the play.

THE JEWS IN THE *PLAY OF ANTICHRIST*

The sympathetic role played by Synagoga and the Jews in the *Play of Antichrist* is unusual and striking enough to merit special attention even in a brief discussion of this drama. To be sure, the twelfth century, when the play was written, is generally regarded as a relatively peaceful and tolerant period in Jewish-Christian relations. The Jews could usually depend on the special protection of the western European monarchs, who needed them to gather revenue for states which as yet had no centrally controlled bureaucracies.[1] The official position of the Church was one of physical toleration coupled with doctrinal opposition. Pope Calixtus II had (*circa* 1120) outlined the rights of the Jews in his bull *Sicut Iudeis non*,[2] and the Third Lateran Council of 1179 called for toleration "on the grounds of humanity alone" (*pro sola humanitate*).[3] As for the position of the Jews in twelfth-century society as a whole, a modern historian has recently stated, "There can be no denying the unifying and unique contribution made by Jewish learning and piety to the intellectual and religious culture of earlier medieval Europe, above all during the twelfth, that most 'open' of the medieval centuries."[4]

The modern student, however, must guard against allowing his admiration for the achievements of twelfth-century civilisation to make him sentimental about its more unpleasant side. For all

---

[1] See G. I. Langmuir, "The Jews and the Archives of Angevin England: Some Reflections on Medieval Anti-Semitism." *Traditio* 19 (1963) 183-244. Though ostensibly just a review of H. G. Richardson's *The English Jewry under Angevin Kings* (London, 1960), this article is by far the best general treatment I have been able to find on the whole question of the position of the Jews in mediaeval society. See also Guido Kisch, *The Jews in Medieval Germany* (Chicago, 1949) and E. A. Synan, *The Popes and the Jews in the Middle Ages* (New York, 1965).

[2] Langmuir 202; for this text and its translation see Synan 229-232.

[3] Friedrich Heer, *The Medieval World*, tr. J. Sondheimer (London, 1962) 256.

[4] *Ibid*. 254.

its accomplishments in literature, music, art, theology and law, the age was largely one of quick and thoughtless violence, of government by brute force; the gentlemanly tolerance so stylish in the nineteenth century was decidedly not one of its characteristics.[5] The protective attitude of royalty towards the Jews was based upon expedience, not principle; furthermore, it implied no respect, but was at best paternalistic in its position that the Jews were almost the personal property of the monarch.[6] As for the Church, the subtleties of its official position were too complex for ordinary clergy and laymen to grasp.[7] Even bishops were powerless to stop the massacres of Jews which accompanied the gathering of the Second Crusade in the Rhineland; the direct intervention of the popular hero St. Bernard was needed.[8] If authors like the German poet Wolfram von Eschenbach confined their attacks on Judaism to statements about its doctrine,[9] others, such as the talented poets of the *Carmina burana*, were already engaged in creating the Jewish stereotype which culminated in Shylock and the Jew of Malta.[10] Thus when we come upon a work like the *Play of Antichrist*, in which Jewish doctrine,

---

[5] Cf. Langmuir 192: "It is difficult to imagine a more perfect screen [than the Jews] on which might be projected the dissatisfactions, the anxieties, the hostility, and the repressed fantasies of the delights and powers of evil brewed by all the tensions of a rapidly developing and increasingly institutionalized society."

[6] See Langmuir 198-202.

[7] Langmuir 235: " ... Christianity could neither live with Judaism nor without it. If the competition of Christianity had hardened Judaism until Jews were almost impervious to the attractions of assimilation, the doctrine elaborated by Christianity to counteract Judaism ensured, by a narrow margin, the continuance of Judaism in an avowedly Christian society."

[8] V. G. Berry, "The Second Crusade," in *A History of the Crusades*, ed. K. M. Setton (Philadelphia, 1955) 1, 472.

[9] Kisch 326.

[10] In the Benediktbeuern Christmas Play from the *Carmina burana* (Karl Young, *The Drama of the Medieval Church* [Oxford, 1933, 1962²] 2, 172-190). It is especially interesting that the *Antichrist* playwright should avoid stereotyping the Jews in his play when we consider that the play gives such early examples of other stereotypes: a Frenchman who is an overly intellectual coward and a German who is noble and brave but not very intelligent.

though of course attacked by a Christian author, is presented with solemnity and respect, and which reaches its climax with the Jews being martyred as the only possessors of the true faith in a depraved world, a close examination of the Jews' role in such a work would certainly seem desirable.

The play opens with what might be called a pageant of the three great faiths. After Gentilitas (Heathendom) sings her song in praise of polytheism, the Jews enter, accompanied by their representative Synagoga, who sings a hymn-like song against the doctrines of trinitarianism and the Incarnation,[11] which begins:

> Lord, our salvation is in Thee;
> In man there is no hope for life.
> To hope that we can ever gain
> Salvation in the name of Christ is vain.   (lines 33-36)

Though of course the *Antichrist* playwright would disagree with the position put forth in this song, he has nevertheless made it seem neither comic nor vicious.

Synagoga and the Jews are silent from this point on throughout that part of the play which deals with the triumph of the Last Roman Emperor. In the play's second half, after all the world including Heathendom has fallen to Antichrist, his messengers approach the Jews. Their speech treats the Jews' exile and their theological position of waiting for the Messiah with sympathy and dignity; the conclusion is resounding:

> Jerusalem, thy light is come: arise!
> Long captive Synagoga, take thy prize!   (lines 317-318)

The Jews fall to Antichrist, of course, since the whole point of the play is that men are powerless against evil without God's help. But God's help is not long in coming: the Prophets Enoch and Elijah suddenly appear; they give the word of God to the Jews, who are immediately converted to the faith and denounce Antichrist. (The Prophets' speech includes the charge of

---

11 A possible source for these songs is the pseudo-Augustinian *Alter-catio Ecclesiae et Synagogae*; see Young 2, 390 and E. K. Chambers, *The Mediaeval Stage* (Oxford, 19544) 2, 64.

"deicide" (line 340), but it is stated baldly, without rancor, and with no suggestion that revenge would be appropriate.) The bold stand of the Jews and the Prophets against Antichrist leads to their immediate execution, while Ecclesia rejoices in the glory of their martyrdom (line 401).

Despite the obvious humanity and sympathy of the *Antichrist* playwright, there remains something of a mystery in the fact that he should allow the Jews alone among all men on earth (the Prophets of course are sent from Heaven) to be the possessors of God's truth at the End of the world. Adso's *Essay on Antichrist* states that Enoch and Elijah will come to defend the "faithful of God" and the "elect"; to be sure, they will also convert whatever Jews they can find, but certainly Adso felt that the vast majority of the "elect" would be Christians.

There are two possible explanations for this discrepancy between Adso and the play. The first is simple dramatic economy. The *Antichrist* playwright had no anonymous Christians in his cast, only kings. Obviously, singling out any particular king to be saved was impossible: such blatant chauvinism would have completely vitiated his play (though the playwright was a patriotic German, his patriotism clearly took second place to his Christianity and his artistic integrity). Since he had no Christians available, he simply did the most economical thing and used the Jews. In a play of such an ecumenical nature, the Jews obviously had to be included in the cast anyway, and their redemption by Enoch and Elijah was, after all, a legitimate part of the Antichrist story as our playwright received it. The other possible explanation of the problem is that the *Antichrist* playwright might have been somewhat inattentive in reading his source. It is not hard to get lost in Adso's careless and disorganised narrative, and that part of it which deals with the conversion of the Jews not only comes right before the all-important description of the martyrdom of Enoch and Elijah but is also embellished with a scriptural quotation. A glance at the translation of Adso's *Essay* which forms an appendix to this work will show how a careless reading of this section might easily lead to the impression that the Jews were the Prophets' only converts. Perhaps both explanations are true: the Jews' conversion is described more memorably in Adso than the

Christians', and the changes the *Antichrist* playwright made in Adso's account make better and simpler drama.

But in spite of all these explanations: a carelessly written source, an improved drama, and the Church's official position of toleration (which we would assume that a monk and cleric — as the *Antichrist* playwright certainly was — would be inclined to follow) — the inescapable fact remains that in his treatment of the Jews the author of the *Play of Antichrist* showed a broadly based, tolerant humanity which for his time, and in fact for most periods in history, is unfortunately very rare.

CONCLUSION

The *Play of Antichrist* stands in isolation in the history of European drama.[1] Despite its excellence it appears to have been forgotten almost as soon as it was written.[2] The playwright's metrical innovations were not imitated; his allegorical figures (like Heresy and Hypocrisy) found no companions in drama until the end of the fourteenth century.[3] Succeeding dramatists did not profit from his clear sense of structure; it is not until much later that we find playwrights with as sure and certain control of plot — and then only with the all-pervasive influence of the rediscovered classical drama as a guide. We cannot even claim that the *Play of Antichrist* had any effect on the development of Latin drama, to say nothing of the vernacular plays that were later to eclipse the Latin drama in western Europe. But the anomalous position of the play in the historical development of literature does not detract from its intrinsic value; viewed from a strictly evolutionary angle, even Shakespeare is a failure, since the drama that followed him was so inferior to his. One historian of the mediaeval drama of England, perhaps rather tired of having his subject continually judged only from the standpoint of what it eventually became, rightly maintains that " ... medieval religious drama existed for itself and for the discharge of a religious purpose and not as an early stage of secular drama."[4] Add "political" to "religious purpose" and this statement applies equally well to the *Play of Antichrist.*

---

[1] Any general statement about mediaeval literature is necessarily based on incomplete evidence. Many works have been lost, and much pertinent material still remains unpublished.

[2] In the Christmas play from the *Carmina burana,* however, there are quotations from the opening song of Gentilitas; see Wilhelm Meyer, *Gesammelte Abhandlungen zur mittellateinischen Rythmik* (Berlin, 1905) 1, 150.

[3] See E. K. Chambers, *The Mediaeval Stage* (Oxford, 1954⁴) 2, 151 and Karl Young, *The Drama of the Medieval Church* (Oxford, 1933, 1962²) 2, 395.

[4] Hardin Craig, *English Religious Drama of the Middle Ages* (Oxford, 1955) 6-7.

To a reader unacquainted with the rest of mediaeval drama, the *Play of Antichrist* will probably seem distressingly primitive. Though other playwrights, such as Aeschylus, sometimes use plots that are even simpler than that of our play, their simplicity of plot is usually balanced by a compensating richness of poetry and thought. Our playwright, by comparison, is rather a competent metrical technician than a poet, and his philosophy never goes beyond a simple and doctrinaire view of politics and religion. This simplicity of ideas and lack of poetry makes it impossible to assign the play to the first rank of European drama. But when we judge it in the light of the time in which it was written, which we must do, by a sort of inner compulsion,[5] the achievement of the *Antichrist* playwright will appear considerable. Compare his major source, Adso's *Essay on Antichrist*, with all its *hysteron proteron* and misplaced emphasis. Few mediaeval playwrights had a more unlikely source from which to draw real drama.[6] Yet the *Antichrist* playwright rearranged and reemphasised, added to and subtracted from the narrative of the *Essay* so effectively that his dramatization of the Antichrist story seems natural and easy. The most superficial examination of the other dramatic accounts of Antichrist, however, will show that this apparent ease is deceptive. The other playwrights used the tradition of Adso if not the *Essay* itself, yet their misplaced sense of the dramatic led them to overemphasise the narrative's obvious opportunities for verbal conflict (for example, a long and blustering theological disputation between Antichrist and the two Prophets[7]), with the result that

[5] Cf. Lionel Trilling, "The Sense of the Past," in *The Liberal Imagination* (New York, 1950) 185: "... the factor of historicity ... is itself a positive aesthetic factor with positive and pleasurable relations to the other aesthetic factors. It is part of the *given* of the work, which we cannot help but respond to."

[6] It has been suggested that there must have been earlier dramatic treatments of the Antichrist theme on which our playwright based his work. See L. U. Lucken, *Antichrist and the Prophets of Antichrist in the Chester Cycle* (Washington, 1940) 27 and Gerhard von Zezschwitz, *Das Drama vom Ende des römischen Kaisertums und von der Erscheinung des Antichrists* (Leipzig, 1878) 11.

[7] In the Chester "Coming of Antichrist," *The Chester Plays* (Early English Text Society E. S. 115, Oxford, 1959³) 412-420.

they come close to reducing their plays to farce.[8] From this we can see that the dignity and significance of the Tegernsee *Antichrist* came not from its sources or from any real or imagined peculiarities of mediaeval thought but rather from the author's own skill as a playwright.

One of the anomalies of the *Antichrist* playwright is his intense sense of nationalism. When we consider that he was writing in the international language of Latin, his emphasis on national pride and superiority is all the more surprising. One historian maintains that not even in the vernacular literature of this period can he find such nationalism on the part of a German author.[9] Since most of the commentary on the play has been produced by German scholars during a period (the late nineteenth century[10]) when reunification was causing national feeling in Germany to run high, the nationalism in the *Play of Antichrist* has been greatly emphasised. But it must not be forgotten that the play's nationalism is still only relative. The playwright's position is basically universal. Although his motives are the highest, the King of the Teutons still falls to Antichrist. Thus the playwright clearly states his belief that all human beings are equally weak in the face of such overwhelming evil.

In fact, its unusual German nationalism notwithstanding, the *Play of Antichrist* for all its simplicity presents a very clear and correct outline of the world order of the High Middle Ages. The modern student of history is apt to concentrate his attention (or at least his approval) on France and England to the detriment of the Holy Roman Empire. The monarchies of France and England were a success from the evolutionary point of view: they produced the two dominant nation-states of modern Western Europe; the Holy Roman Empire, on the other hand, was a

---

[8] Such realistic and almost farcical touches, however, were very important for the development of realistic drama; see chapter 7, "Adam and Eve," in Erich Auerbach's *Mimesis: The Representation of Reality in Western Literature,* tr. Willard Trask (Princeton, 1953).

[9] Karl Langosch, *Politische Dichtung um Kaiser Friedrich Barbarossa* (Berlin, 1943) 78.

[10] The work by Langosch cited above was written in 1943, when German nationalism was of course even more rampant than in the nineteenth century.

failure, producing nothing but dry rot that had to be removed before Germany, Italy, and the nations of Eastern Europe could come into their own. But for the twelfth-century Christian, Rome and the Holy Roman Empire were the center of the world. Though they often chafed at the bit, the kings of France and England would usually acknowledge the primacy (if not the practical sovereignty) of the Holy Roman Emperor, and the time was soon to come when the pope's temporal power would be so great that even far-off England would be his vassal. Catholicism, in both senses of the word, was still the dominant ideology, not nationalism. And the *Play of Antichrist*, despite the obvious quality of wishful thinking connected with its portrayal of the universal power of the Empire, gives us a faithful picture of this world order.

The *Play of Antichrist* was produced at the height of what has been called the Renaissance of the Twelfth Century.[11] The term is correct in two senses. The scholars of this period, though hampered by their ignorance of Greek, produced a real renaissance in the narrow sense: a revival of the study and appreciation of classical literature. The twelfth century was a renaissance in the broader, historical sense as well. It was a time of great political expansion for Christendom: the Holy Land was conquered; peaceful contacts with the East were broadened; missionaries and crusaders were at work enlarging the area of Christian rule in the east and north of Europe. The greatest architecture ever produced by man had its immediate origins in the twelfth century: Chartres and Notre Dame, for example, were begun at this time. The mediaeval Latin lyric, religious and secular, was reaching its highest point; theology and law were moving rapidly to their greatest development. In short, it was an age which seemed to promise the fulfilment of all that Latin Christendom represented: a unified civilisation; theology, law, art, sculpture, and architecture communally or anonymously created and devoted to the greater glory of God and a hierarchical world order, a largely anonymous creative

[11] Notably by C. H. Haskins, *The Renaissance of the Twelfth Century* (New York, 1959²).

literature written in an international language that any educated
man could understand, and an educational system which, thanks
to this same language, possessed such a spirit of scholarly inter-
nationalism as to be almost incredible when we consider the
physical difficulties which hampered communication at that time.
But this world order, celebrated so well in the Tegernsee *Antichrist* with its plot, its structure, its political and religious ideas,
with the very language in which it is written, was soon to come
to an end. Literary study was to give way to scholasticism, Latin
literature to the vernacular, anonymous Gothic art to personal,
individualistic creations, the vision of a unified political order to
nationalism, and the universal Church to the schisms of the
Reformation. The self-confident, expansive spirit of the twelfth
century was replaced by a fearful inward withdrawal which led
to the mass hysteria of witch-hunts and anti-Semitism of later
centuries. But even though the author of the *Play of Antichrist*
would undoubtedly have been distressed by these changes,
perhaps he would not have been too surprised. He was clearly
convinced of the impermanence of human accomplishments; in
the words of one of the major sources for the eschatology of
the Last Things,

> ... you yourselves know perfectly that the day of the
> Lord so cometh as a thief in the night. For when they shall
> say, Peace and safety; then sudden destruction cometh upon
> them, as travail upon a woman with child; and they shall not
> **escape.**   (1 Thess. 5.2-3)

THE PLAY OF ANTICHRIST

Scene: The Temple of the Lord and seven royal seats[1] arranged in the following manner: to the east the Temple of the Lord; around it are arranged the seat of the King of Jerusalem and the seat of Synagoga. To the west the seat of the Emperor of the Romans; around it are arranged the seat of the King of the Teutons and the seat of the King of the Franks. To the south the seat of the King of the Greeks. To the south the seat of the King of Babylonia and of Gentilitas. When the scene is set, Gentilitas and the King of Babylonia step forward to start the play. Gentilitas sings:[2]

> The deathless gods must be adored
>   in every mortal rite
> And everywhere their multitudes
>   be fearful in their might.
>
> Men who claim that God is one   5
>   and disregard the rules
> Which all antiquity obeyed
>   are simpletons and fools.

---

[1] See the Introduction under "Staging" for various theories concerning the arrangement of the stage.

[2] Gentilitas's theology in the play is rather confused. In the following song, and elsewhere (see 117 ff., 291 ff.), she defends polytheism, but she is also (298) accused of idol-worship. She presumably also represents the Moslems, who were, of course, monotheistic.

For if we say a single god
    controls the universe,   10
We must admit the forces that
    control him are diverse.

Sometimes he grants a blessed peace
    with loving gentleness;
Sometimes he shakes the storms of war   15
    with savage ruthlessness.

The many different provinces
    the gods must oversee
To us are certain evidence
    of their variety.   20

But those who say a single god
    controls such different forces
Thus have a god whose unity
    is turned in different courses.

Lest then we say a single god   25
    is subject to such friction,
And thus admit divinity
    is ruled by contradiction,

We are determined for this cause
    to separate the gods,   30
Since by their provinces we see
    how much they are at odds.

This should be sung throughout the play from time to time;[3] and so Gentilitas and the King of Babylonia ascend to their seats. Then Synagoga enters with the Jews singing:

[3] This repetition is also suggested for the next song. Perhaps these songs are the ones that are to be "sung by turns" in the rubric which follows line 150.

Lord, our salvation is in Thee;[4]
In man there is no hope for life.
To hope that we can ever gain   35
Salvation in the name of Christ is vain.

Strange, that He should fall to death
Who offered life to other men.
Is one who could not even save
Himself, to rescue others from the grave?   40

As Ishmael despised the gods,
So you are to detest this Christ.
Not He, but Lord Immanuel
Shall be the God adored by Israel.

She will also sing this song from time to time. Synagoga
ascends to her throne. Then Ecclesia enters, dressed in
woman's garments and wearing a breastplate and crown;[5]
escorting her are Mercy, on the right, with oil, and Justice,
on the left, with scales and a sword. Both are dressed in
women's garments. From the right-hand side the Pope[6]
follows her with the Clergy and from the left the Emperor
of the Romans with his army. Ecclesia sings the processional
chant *Alto consilio,*[7] with those who follow her responding
to the individual verses thus:

4 Cf. Jeremiah 3.23: "Truly in the Lord our God is the salvation of
Israel." (All parallel references to the Bible in these notes — for which
I have used the KJV, since its text is the most familiar in English — have
been taken from the edition of the play in Karl Young, *The Drama of the
Medieval Church* [Oxford, 1962²] 2, 371-387.)

5 A practical note on costuming which indicates that the play was
written with actual production in mind. For other directions as to
costume see the rubrics after lines 150 and 186.

6 See the Introduction under "Historical Background" for suggestions as
to why the Pope has such a minor role in the play.

7 "No appropriate hymn or trope beginning *Alto consilio* has been
found." Young 2, 373n; see his references.

This is the faith where life is found,   45
In which the law of death is bound.[8]
Whoever from our faith rebel
We damn eternally to Hell.

She ascends, accompanied by the Pope and the Clergy,[9] and the Emperor and his army, to her throne. Afterwards other kings enter with their armies, individually singing whatever seems to be convenient;[10] and so each and every one ascends his throne with his army; at this point the Temple and one throne remain vacant.[11] The Emperor then directs his messengers to each king, beginning with the King of the Franks, saying:

The writings of historians tell us[12]
That once the whole world was a Roman fief.   50
The strength of early men accomplished this,
But the neglect of their successors squandered it.
Though under them the imperial power fell
The majesty of our might shall win it back.
Therefore each king must henceforth pay to Rome   55
The tribute that was previously set.

---

8 Cf. Romans 8.2: "For the law of the Spirit of life in Christ Jesus hath made me free from the law of sin and death."

9 Presumably all of these characters are placed on the Emperor's platform.

10 The "other kings" are the King of the Franks, the King of the Greeks, and the King of Jerusalem. See Langosch's text and translation in *Geistliche Spiele* (Berlin, 1957²) 179-239, for suggestions as to what songs would be appropriate for these characters to sing.

11 This is the "seat of the King of the Teutons" mentioned in the opening rubric; it will be occupied by the Emperor after he surrenders his crown to God.

12 Here and in line 64 the reference is to the newly revived Roman law, according to which the Roman Emperor was *dominus mundi*; see Introduction under "Historical Background."

But since the Frankish race is strong in war,
Their king may serve the Empire in arms.
He must do homage and swear fealty
Before his Emperor: that is our decree.[13]   60

Then the Ambassadors, coming to the King of the Franks,
sing before him:

The Emperor of the Romans sends his greetings
To his renowned ally, the Frankish King.
We trust, your grace, that you already know
You are obliged to bow to Roman law
Whence the decision of supreme empire,   65
Forever binding and forever feared,
Now seeks you out. Therefore we summon you
Into the Emperor's service,[14] and we demand
That you come quickly under his command.

To them he replies:

If anyone can trust historians,
This Empire has no hold on us, but rather   70
It is ours, since the Gauls possessed it once,
And left it to us as their legacy.[15]
A thieving army comes to rob it now,
But brigands' threats will never make us bow.

13 The Emperor's relations with the other kings follow the forms of
mediaeval vassalage very precisely. Here, the Emperor demands that the
King of the Franks pay him homage (*hominium*) and take an oath of
fealty (*fidelitas*). See F. L. Ganshof, *Feudalism,* tr. Philip Grierson (New
York, 1961²) 69-105.
14 The Latin word used here is *servitium,* which was the common term
for the vassal's military service to his lord. See Ganshof 87.
15 Here the reference is to the French claim that the Roman Empire
was really the possession of the French, rather than the German kings.
See Introduction under "Historical Background" and Adso 1295: "Indeed,

Then the Ambassadors, returning to the Emperor, sing before him:

> Behold how haughtily the proud Franks boast,[16]   75
> Boldly flaunting all your majesty.
> They undermine the Empire's legal rule
> While they pretend your claim is robbery.
> So let them taste the wrath of your great sway;
> Their fate will teach the others to obey.   80

Then the Emperor sings:

> A haughty spirit goes before a fall; [17]
> No wonder fools speak such great swelling words.[18]
> We surely shall destroy these rebels' pride
> And trample them beneath our feet.[19] And those
> Who do not wish as vassals[20] to obey   85
> Will learn to serve as slaves some other day.

And immediately he sets out with his army to attack the King of the Franks. They meet in battle, and the Frankish King is conquered and brought as a captive to the seat of

---

certain of our learned men tell us that one of the kings of the Franks, who will come very soon, will possess the Roman Empire in its entirety." (References to Adso in these notes are by the column numbers of Migne's edition, which are reproduced in square brackets in my translation of the *Essay on Antichrist* in the Appendix.)

16 I have followed Meyer's emendation of *superbi* for *super te.*

17 Cf. Proverbs 16.18: "Pride goeth before destruction, and an haughty spirit before a fall."

18 Cf. 2 Peter 2.18: "For when they speak such great swelling words of vanity."

19 Cf. Lamentations of Jeremiah 3.34: "To crush under his feet all the prisoners of the earth."

20 *Miles* (lit. "soldier") was a common technical term for vassal; see Ganshof 69.

the Emperor. As the Emperor sits, he stands before him
and sings:

> The glory of a victor is to spare
> His conquered foes, and, conquered, I now
> Obey your least command. I know my life
> And royal dignity are in your hands.   90
> But if you let me keep my royal crown,
> This kind deed will bring you great renown.

The Emperor then, accepting his homage,[21] and permitting
him to keep his kingdom, sings:

> Live through my grace, and keep your royal name,
> Since you acknowledge my imperial claim.

The Frankish King is dismissed with honor and returns to
his kingdom, singing:

> We venerate the glory of Rome's name,   95
> And we are proud to serve Augustus Caesar.
> The power of his Empire is supreme;
> Let his fame and honor be forever feared.
> We recognise your imperial sovereignty;
> We follow your command whole-heartedly.[22]   100

Then the Emperor directs his messengers to the King of the
Greeks, saying:

21 Lat.: *eum suscipiens in hominem*: the essential ritual for the act of
homage was the *immixtio manuum*: "the vassal, generally kneeling, bare-
headed and weaponless, placed his clasped hands between the hands of his
lord, who closed his own hands over them" (Ganshof 73). The rubric
indicates that this rite was performed on the stage.

22 This speech appears to be a versification of the second part of the
act of homage, the *volo* ("declaration of intention") usually expressed in
such terms as *devenio homo vester* ("I become your vassal"). Ganshof *ibid.*

The writings of historians tell us
That once the whole world was a Roman fief.
The strength of early men accomplished this,
But the neglect of their successors squandered it.
Though under them the imperial power fell   105
The majesty of our might shall win it back.
Therefore each king must henceforth pay to Rome
The tribute that was previously set.
Now go to the Greeks with this decree;
Bring back the tribute that they owe to me.[23]   110

They come to the Greek King and sing before him:

The Emperor of the Romans sends his greetings[24]   110a
To his renowned ally, the King of Greece.
We trust, your grace, that you already know
You are obliged to bow to Roman law
Whence the decision of supreme empire,
Forever binding and forever feared,
Now seeks you out. Therefore we summon you
Into the Emperor's service, and command   111
You pay at once the tribute we demand.

He nobly acknowledges their request, singing:

We venerate the glory of Rome's name,
And we are proud to serve Augustus Caesar.
The power of his Empire is supreme;

---

[23] The *servitium* of the King of the Greeks (and later of the King of Jerusalem) consists not of military service but of a payment of money; this was a common feudal practice. (Ganshof 90-91)

[24] From this point in the MS on, all repetitions are indicated simply by the first phrase of the song followed by "et cetera." (Changed lines are, of course, written out.) I have copied out all the repeated speeches in full in order to show the effect they would have in performance.

Let his fame and honor be forever feared.
We recognise your imperial sovereignty;
We follow your command whole-heartedly.

And dismissing them with honor he himself goes to the
Emperor's throne singing the same song. The Emperor,
accepting his homage and permitting him to keep his
kingdom, sings:

Live through my grace, and keep your royal name 114b
Since you acknowledge my imperial claim.

And after the King of the Greeks has received his kingdom,
he returns singing:

We venerate the glory of Rome's name,   114c
And we are proud to serve Augustus Caesar.
The power of his Empire is supreme;
Let his fame and honor be forever feared.
We recognise your imperial sovereignty;
We follow your command whole-heartedly.

Then again the Emperor directs his messengers to the King
of Jerusalem, saying:

The writings of historians tell us   114d
That once the whole world was a Roman fief.
The strength of early men accomplished this,
But the neglect of their successors squandered it.
Though under them the imperial power fell
The majesty of our might shall win it back.
Therefore each king must henceforth pay to Rome
The tribute that was previously set.
Go to Jerusalem with this decree;
Bring back the tribute that they owe to me.

They come to the King and sing before him:

> The Emperor of the Romans sends his greetings   115
> To his ally, the King of Jerusalem.
> We trust, your grace, that you already know
> You are obliged to bow to Roman law
> Whence the decision of supreme empire,
> Forever binding and forever feared,
> Now seeks you out. Therefore we summon you
> Into the Emperor's service, and command
> You pay at once the tribute we demand.

The King of Jerusalem nobly acknowledges their request, singing:

> We venerate the glory of Rome's name,   116a
> And we are proud to serve Augustus Caesar.
> The power of his Empire is supreme;
> Let his fame and honor be forever feared.
> We recognise your imperial sovereignty;
> We follow your command whole-heartedly.

And ascending to the imperial seat, he repeats the same song. The Emperor accepts his homage and grants him his kingdom. When he returns to his seat the whole Christian world is subject to the Roman Empire.[25] The King of Babylonia stands up in the midst of his subjects and sings:

> Behold this worship of vain novelty.
> How far from truth this Christian cult has strayed!
> It has by now almost destroyed the rites

---

[25] For "the whole Christian world" the Latin reads *tota ecclesia*. For the legend of the universal rule of the Last Roman Emperor see the Introduction under "Legendary Background" and cf. Adso 1295: "Indeed, certain of our learned men tell us that one of the kings of the Franks, who will come very soon, will possess the Roman Empire in its entirety. And he will be the greatest and last of all kings."

Of old, and has dethroned the ancient gods.   120
Their worship will be utterly destroyed
Unless we wipe the Christian name from earth.
Therefore, to start our work, we ought to go
To the country where this sect began to grow.

And, marshalling his army, he goes to attack Jerusalem.[26]
Then the King of Jerusalem directs his messengers to the
Emperor, telling them:

Go, report these evils to the Church   125
And seek assistance from her for our land.
As soon as the Emperor of the Romans knows
These facts, he will protect us from our foes.

The messengers come to the Emperor and sing before him:

Have pity, O Defender of the Church,
On us, whom God's own foes wish to destroy.   130
The heathen are come into God's inheritance;[27]
They hold His holy city under siege.
That land, which once His holy presence graced,
Their godless band intends to see debased.

To them he says:

Go, console your brothers straightaway;   135
Let them rejoice that they have sought our aid.
For we shall soon be standing by their side,
To smite God's enemies, and stem their pride.

---

26 This attack on Jerusalem by the "King of Babylonia" is probably a
reflection of the pressure being brought to bear by the Moslems on the
Latin Kingdom of Jerusalem at the time the play was being written; see
Introduction under "Historical Background."

27 Cf. Psalm 79.1: "O God, the heathen are come into thine
inheritance."

They return and stand before the King singing:

> Fight on against the foe; be not dismayed,[28]
> For help from the Emperor is at hand.   140
> Be firm in battle; wait for him; soon he
> Will joyfully restore your liberty.

While the Emperor marshals his troops, an Angel of the Lord,[29] appearing suddenly, sings:

> Judea and Jerusalem, fear not.
> Know that tomorrow you shall see God's aid.
> To set you free your brothers are at hand   145
> And they shall drive the enemy from your land.

Then a Chorus:[30]

> Judea and Jerusalem,[31] fear not; tomorrow go out   146a
> against them, and the Lord will be with you.
> R : Be steadfast: you will see the help of the
> Lord above you.

Meanwhile, the Emperor and his men advance to battle, and, when the Chorus's responsory is finished, they attack

---

[28] Cf. 1 Chron. 28.20: "Fear not, nor be dismayed."

[29] This and the crack of thunder which ends the reign of Antichrist are the only two instances of the *deus ex machina* in the play. The appearance of the angel underscores the dignity and the universal importance of the rescue of Jerusalem by the armies of Christendom.

[30] This is the only appearance of the Chorus. Despite the importance of this moment in the play, it is difficult, though not impossible, to imagine a whole chorus' being kept on the stage throughout the play only to sing a single responsory. Perhaps the Chorus was a single actor.

[31] The text reads *Tunc chorus: Iudea et Ierusalem.* Young (2, 376) suggests that the use of the word "responsorio" in the next rubric and the musical notation found in the MS over the words *Iudea et Ierusalem* indicate that at this point a responsory, the text of which he quotes from *Antiphonale du B. Hartker, Paléographie musicale* 2 Ser. 1 (Solesmes, 1900) 7, was to be sung. I have translated this responsory and inserted it here.

the King of Babylonia; when he is defeated and in flight, the Emperor and his men enter the Temple. The Emperor worships there; then, taking his crown from his head, he places it, along with a sceptre and his imperial dignity, before the altar, singing:

> Receive, O Lord, my grateful gift, for I
> Resign my rule to Thee, the King of Kings,
> Through Whom kings reign,[32] and Whom alone we call
> The Emperor and Ruler of us all.   150

He places these gifts on the altar, and returns to the seat of his ancient kingdom.[33] Ecclesia, who had come with him to Jerusalem, remains in the Temple. Then, while Ecclesia and Gentilitas and Synagoga sing by turns as above,[34] the Hypocrites enter, silently, and, bowing their heads everywhere with a show of humility, they win over the favor of the laity.[35] Finally, they all gather together before Ecclesia and the seat of the King of Jerusalem, who receives them into fealty and submits himself entirely to their counsel. Immediately Antichrist enters, dressed in a breastplate which is hidden under his other garments.[36] Accompanying

[32] Cf. Proverbs 8.15: "By me kings reign."

[33] This surrender of the Empire to God ends the reign of the Last Roman Emperor. See Adso 1295: "He [the Emperor], after governing his kingdom prosperously, will ultimately come to Jerusalem and lay down his sceptre and crown on Mount Olivet. This will be the end and the consummation of the Empire of the Romans and the Christians."

[34] These are probably the songs sung at the opening of the play. See note 3 above.

[35] This and the action described in the rubric following line 170 are early examples of the dumb show, a stage technique that later became quite popular.

[36] See Adso 1295: "And immediately [after the Last Emperor surrenders his crown], according to the aforesaid opinion of the Apostle Paul, they say that Antichrist will soon be at hand...."

him are Hypocrisy on the right and Heresy on the left, to
whom he sings:

> The hour of my reign is here;[37]
> Therefore you both must persevere;
> Prepare at once the way for me
> To mount the throne of royalty.
> I wish the world to adore
> Myself alone forevermore.
> You both are apt for this, I know;   155
> I raised you for it long ago.
> Now is the time when I must ask
> Your help and labor for this task.
> Behold, the nations all enthrone,
> Revere, and worship Christ alone.   160
> Therefore, wipe out His memory,
> And transfer His renown to me.

To Hypocrisy:

> In you the groundwork I will lay.

To Heresy:

> Through you the later growth will come.

To Hypocrisy:

> Through you the faithful then will stray.   165

To Heresy:

> Through you the clergy will succumb.

---

[37] The importance of Antichrist's appearance is emphasized by a
change in meter; see Introduction under "Rhythm and Music."

They reply:

> We'll place the world's faith in you;
> The name of Christ we will subdue.

Hypocrisy:

> The faithful will believe you, through my work.

Heresy:

> And Christ denied, through me, by every clerk.   170

Then they set out, while he follows a little way behind. And after they come before the seat of the King of Jerusalem, Hypocrisy, whispering to the Hypocrites, announces to them the advent of Antichrist. They rush up to him at once, singing:

> The holy faith has limped for many years,
> And vanity has captured Mother Church.
> And to what purpose is this waste,[38] these men
> Adorned? God loves not worldly priests.[39]
> Arise, then: ascend the royal height   175
> To change these worn-out relics with your might.

Then Antichrist:

> How shall this be? I am an unknown man.

---

[38] Cf. Matt. 26.8: "To what purpose is this waste?"
[39] This attack by the Hypocrites on "worldly priests" (or "secular clergy"; the Latin pun cannot be translated) appears to reflect the conflict between the secular clergy of the Holy Roman Empire and papalist reformers like Gerhoh of Reichersberg; see Introduction under "Historical Background."

They reply:

> The whole world will support you, thanks to us.
> We have won the faithful's trust, and now
> Through you the clergy's learning soon will fall.   180
> With our aid now you occupy this throne.
> The rest will come through skills that are your own.

Then Antichrist comes before the seat of the King of Jerusalem and sings to the Hypocrites:

> Once you conceived me in the Church's womb,
> And after many hardships gave me birth.
> Therefore, I now shall conquer all the lands,   185
> Throw out the old, and lay down new commands.

Then, laying aside their robes, they advance with drawn swords; they depose the King of Jerusalem and crown Antichrist, singing:

> Strong is thy hand, and high is thy right hand.[40]   186a

Then the King of Jerusalem ascends alone to the seat of the King of the Teutons, singing:

> The men I thought were good have cheated me;
> Behold: I am betrayed by these dissemblers.
> I thought our kingdom's happiness complete
> Once set in order by our holy laws.   190
> With you, the Roman Emperor, as her guard,
> The Holy Church was held in high esteem.
> Your abdication clearly then was wrong,
> For deadly heresy is growing strong.

---

[40] Quoted directly from Psalm 89.13.

Meanwhile the Hypocrites lead Antichrist into the Temple
of the Lord and place his throne there.[41] Ecclesia, who had
remained there despite insults and blows, returns to the
seat of the Pope. Antichrist then sends his messengers[42] to
each king, beginning with the King of the Greeks.[43] He
tells his messengers:

> You know that Heaven has given me to you   195
> To hold a princely power through every land.
> So I have made you able ministers[44]
> To place the entire world beneath our law.
> Go seize the land of Greece without delay;
> Use force or fear to make the Greeks obey.[45]   200

They go to the King of the Greeks and sing before him:

> Your majesty, our Saviour, King of Kings
> And Lord of all this world, sends his greetings.
> He now, as promised by the Holy Writ,
> Descends from Heaven, sent from the Father's throne.[46]
> The everlasting God, he summons us   205
> To life, through his paternal holiness.
> He wishes to be recognised as God

---

41 See Adso 1293: "Then he [Antichrist] will come to Jerusalem, and all
the Christians whom he cannot convert to his side he will kill by various
torments, and he will place his own throne in the holy temple."

42 Antichrist seems to have had no separate messengers; rather, he used
the Hypocrites for this purpose. See the rubric following line 218.

43 See Adso 1293: "He [Antichrist] will first convert kings and princes
to his side and then, through them, the rest of the people."

44 Cf. 2 Cor. 3.6: "Who also hath made us able ministers of the new
testament."

45 See Adso 1294: "Those whom he [Antichrist] cannot corrupt by gifts,
he will conquer by fear."

46 A responsory (Hartker 45) and the fourth stanza of Fortunatus's
hymn *Pange lingua* might have influenced this line; see Young 2, 379.

By all; he demands the whole world's worship.
If you decide to disobey our lord,
You and your realm will perish by the sword.   210

To them he says:

I freely grant my service to the King
Whom you declare is now so nobly raised.
Obeying such a leader honors me;
I long to follow him whole-heartedly.

Repeating this, he goes to Antichrist and stands before him
singing:

I acknowledge your imperial right;
I ask to serve you as a royal knight.

And he bends his knee and offers him his crown. Then
Antichrist paints the first letter of his name[47] on the foreheads of the King and all his men, and replaces the crown
on the King's head, singing:

Live through my grace, and keep your royal name,
Since you have recognised my godhead's claim.

The King of the Greeks then returns to his seat. Antichrist
next directs the Hypocrites to the King of the Franks with
gifts for him,[48] saying:

Offer these presents to the Frankish King,
And win his nation over to our side.   220
These men already worship by our rites

---

[47] See Adso 1297: "And whoever believes in him [Antichrist] will
receive the sign of his letter upon his forehead."
[48] See Adso 1294: "To those who believe in him, he [Antichrist] will
give great presents of gold and silver."

And have prepared the way for our advent.[49]
We were enabled, through their subtle wit,[50]
To mount the throne where virtue used to sit.

Then the Hypocrites take the gifts and go to the King of
the Franks. Standing before him they sing:

Your majesty, our Saviour, King of Kings,   224a
And Lord of all this world, sends his greetings.
He now, as promised by the Holy Writ,
Descends from Heaven, sent from the Father's throne.
The everlasting God, he summons us
To life, through his paternal holiness.
He wishes to be recognised as God
By all; he demands the whole world's worship.
But since you are devoted to him still,   225
He now repays the gift of your good will.

The King takes the gifts and sings:

I freely grant my service to the King   226a
Whom you declare is now so nobly raised.
Obeying such a leader honors me;
I long to follow him whole-heartedly.

Repeating this song in the presence of Antichrist, the King
bends his knee and offers him his crown, singing:

I acknowledge your imperial right;   226b
I ask to serve you as a royal knight.

49 Cf. Isaiah 62.10: "Prepare ye the way of the people."
50 It has been suggested that these lines refer to the subtle theological
speculation of Peter Abelard; see Eduard Michaelis, "Zum Ludus de
Antichristo," *Zeitschrift für deutsches Altertum* 54 (1913) 82.

Antichrist, accepting his homage, kisses him[51] and puts his mark on the foreheads of him and his men; he places the crown on the King's head, singing:

> Live through my grace, and keep your royal name,   226c
> Since you have recognised my godhead's claim.

Antichrist next directs the Hypocrites to the King of the Teutons, singing:

> The Teutons are a mighty race in war,[52]
> As those will witness who have felt their wrath.
> We have to pacify their King with gifts;
> To battle with the Teutons is unwise.   230
> These savages are the ruin of those they fight,
> So conquer them with gifts instead of might.

The Hypocrites take the gifts, go to the King, and sing before him:

> Your majesty, our Saviour, King of kings,   232a
> And Lord of all this world, sends his greetings.
> He now, as promised by the Holy Writ,
> Descends from Heaven, sent from the Father's throne.
> The everlasting God, he summons us
> To life, through his paternal holiness.
> He wishes to be recognised as God

---

[51] The ceremonial kiss (*osculum*) was an addition to the rite of homage and fealty; it was not essential to the vassalage contract, but "simply a way of confirming the obligations contracted by the two parties ... a sort of analogy to it is the drink or hand-clasp by which a bargain is still often sealed today." (Ganshof 78.) Its use at this point of course emphasises the close connection between Antichrist and the King of the Franks.

[52] Nationalistic notes such as this one and the reference to national honor in 271 are balanced in the play by the fact that it is the gullibility of the King of the Teutons which leads to his seduction by Antichrist.

By all; he demands the whole world's worship.
He honors you with gifts, though far away;
He longs to see you close to him some day.

Then the King of the Teutons sings:

I am compelled to test these clever frauds;   235
Your evil hearts have always told me lies.
We think we see the truth, in virtue's form,
But when the mask is off, the lie appears.
You have corrupted every Christian's faith,
But I shall destroy your kingdom of deceit.   240
The gifts of this deceiver are a hoax.
My foes shall fall by my avenging sword.
Thy money perish with thee;[53] as for him —
My vengeance for his insult shall be grim.

The Hypocrites return in confusion, and standing before
Antichrist they sing:

O glorious lord, master of all the world,   245
Look on the outrage of this maddened race.
The faith of ancient times has long foretold
That you will surely crush each rebel's pride.
If all the world stands beneath your rule,
By what strength will this German madness last? 250
Germany blasphemes your sovereignty
And takes up arms against the holy faith.
Now look upon our terror, and by this
Pass judgment on the outrage they have done.
Your might is tested by their King's disdain;   255
He threatens to destroy your whole domain.

[53] Cf. Acts 8.20: "Thy money perish with thee."

Then Antichrist:

> I surely shall destroy this outcast race
> For such effrontery to our holy faith.
> Behold, the majesty of godly might
> Shall put the pride of human power to flight.   260

Then he sends a messenger to each of the kings, telling them:

> Go, call together all our royal host;
> They will trample down this prideful boast.

The messengers come before the kings and sing:

> Behold, our royal master, God of Gods,[54]
> Has sent us out to summon all his men.
> To help him stem this mad Teutonic flood   265
> Martyrs in war must shed their holy blood.

The kings meet before the throne of Antichrist. He says to them:

> I surely shall destroy this outcast race   266a
> For such effrontery to our holy faith.
> Behold, the majesty of godly might
> Shall put the pride of human power to flight.
> Take all your men; attack the German foe,
> And lay this haughty King and people low.

Then they all sing:

> God is with us;[55] He will be our shield;
> With trusting hearts for Him we take the field.   270

---

[54] Cf. Dan. 2.47: "That your God is a God of gods."
[55] Cf. Joshua 22.31: "This day we perceive that the Lord is among us."

They marshal their armies and fight with the Teutons. The army of Antichrist is defeated. The King of the Teutons returns and sits on his throne, singing:

Bloodshed must preserve our country's honor,
And valor drive out all her enemies.
Blood alone redeems a tainted name,
And blood will keep the Empire free from shame.

Then the Hypocrites bring a lame man to Antichrist.[56] When Antichrist heals him, the King of the Teutons wavers in his faith. Then they bring a leper; when he is made clean, the King doubts even more. Finally they carry in a coffin, in which a man lies pretending to have been killed in a battle.[57] Antichrist commands him to rise, saying:

Such signs to foolish doubters must be shown;   275
Arise at once, and who I am, make known.[58]

Then he sings from the coffin:

With wisdom and with godly verity
You are unconquered in your majesty.

[56] See Adso 1293-4: "He [Antichrist] will also make many signs, great and unheard-of miracles .... He will even bring the dead to life in the sight of men, 'so that if it were possible, even the elect would be deceived.' For when they see so many great miracles, even those who are righteous and chosen by God will wonder whether or not he is the Christ who, according to the Scriptures, will come at the end of the world."

[57] It is difficult to see how it could have been shown dramatically that the man was *pretending* to have been killed, but at any rate by this rubric the playwright neatly sidesteps the controversy over whether or not Antichrist would really be able to raise the dead. (For this controversy see L. U. Lucken, *Antichrist and the Prophets of Antichrist in the Chester Cycle* [Washington, 1940] 64).

[58] See Matt. 12.39: "An evil and adulterous generation seeketh after a sign" and Acts 12.7: "Arise up quickly."

The Hypocrites sing the same song with him. Then the King of the Teutons, seeing the miracle, is seduced and says:

> We have imperilled ourselves by our attack;
> We were insane to fight against the Lord.   280
> Through his power he brought the dead to life;
> He cleansed the lepers, and he healed the lame;[59]
> Therefore we venerate his holy name.[60]

Singing this song, the King ascends to the throne of Antichrist. When he has come before him, he bends his knee and offers him his crown, singing:

> I acknowledge your imperial right;   284a
> I ask to serve you as a royal knight.

Then Antichrist puts his mark on the foreheads of the King and his men, and replaces the crown on the King's head, singing :

> Live through my grace, and keep your royal name, 284b
> Since you have recognised my godhead's claim.

Then he entrusts to him the expedition against the heathen, saying:

> Since you are saved, we turn to heathendom.   285

And he gives him a sword, singing :

> We trust you to make converts of them all.

The King comes to the throne of Gentilitas, and sends an

---

59 Cf. Matt. 10.8: "Heal the sick, cleanse the lepers."
60 The text has no line to rhyme with this one; therefore, it is probable that a line is missing. See Young 2, 382.

ambassador to the King of Babylonia, who stands before him and sings:

> The power of our Lord continueth ever;[61]
> His is the only will to be obeyed.
> He utterly condemns idolatry.
> The end of heathen rites is his decree. 290

Then Gentilitas says to the ambassador:

> This unity is envy's wild dream
> To force a man to worship but one god.
> Your Lord despises other gods, so now
> He orders us to worship him alone.
> But we will not forsake our worship thus: 295
> Each god will have his sacrifice from us.

Then the ambassador says:

> You must adore our Lord, by Heaven's decree,
> The only God.

And throwing down the image, he sings:

> We hate this effigy.

Immediately the heathen rush together and fight with the army of Antichrist; the King of Babylonia is defeated and led a captive to Antichrist. Then the King bends his knee and offers his crown to Antichrist, saying:

> I acknowledge your imperial right; 298a
> I ask to serve you as a royal knight.

---

61 Cf. Heb. 7.24: "But this man, because he continueth ever, hath an unchangeable priesthood."

Then Antichrist puts his mark on the foreheads of the King
and his men, and replaces the crown on the King's head,
singing:

> Live through my grace, and keep your royal name, 298b
> Since you have recognised my godhead's claim.

At once they all return to their seats singing:

> We recognise your imperial sovereignty;
> We follow your command whole-heartedly. 300

Then Antichrist directs the Hypocrites to Synagoga, telling
them:

> Go tell the Jews the Messiah now is come;
> The gentiles have already welcomed me.
> So tell the Jewish nation, I am he,
> The Messiah long foretold in prophecy.[62]

Then the Hypocrites say to Synagoga:

> The Lord thy God has chosen thee to be 305
> A special people;[63] you have kept His faith.
> Because you kept the Law, you are exiles,
> Far from your home, awaiting the Messiah.
> Your birthright is returned as your reward;
> Old sorrows will be traded for new joys. 310
> Behold the mystery of your redemption;[64]
> For now a King is born to lead your faith.

---

[62] See Adso 1296: "[Antichrist] will circumcise himself, saying to the
Jews, 'I am the Christ promised to you, who am come for your salvation,
to gather together and protect you who were dispersed'."

[63] Cf. Deut. 7.6: "The Lord thy God hath chosen thee to be a special
people unto himself."

[64] Cf. 1 Cor. 15.51: "Behold, I shew you a mystery."

He is Emmanuel, whom Holy Writ
Foretold; through his grace you shall reign secure.
He will exalt the humble, and crush the proud,   315
For he hath put all things beneath his feet.[65]
Jerusalem, thy light is come; arise![66]
Long captive Synagoga, take thy prize!

Then Synagoga says:

The comfort of God's good has looked upon
The labor of our long captivity.   320
Let us receive our Lord with deference;
It is right to show him reverence.

Then Synagoga rises and goes to Antichrist,[67] singing:

You are here, O Lord Emmanuel,
Whose glory is a crown to Israel.

Then Antichrist accepts Synagoga, puts his mark on her, and says:

Bring order to this world in my name;   325
I now restore the promised land to you.
Behold: all nations shall walk in your light;
Beneath your law all kings shall wield their might.

When Synagoga has returned, the Prophets enter,[68] saying:

---

65 Cf. 1 Cor. 15.26: "For he hath put all things under his feet."

66 Cf. Isaiah 60.1: "Arise, shine; for thy light is come."

67 See Adso 1296: "Then all the Jews will rush together to him [Antichrist], thinking that they are accepting God, but they will be accepting the devil."

68 See Adso 1296: "But lest Antichrist come suddenly and without warning and deceive and destroy the whole human race at once by his error, before his arrival two great prophets, Enoch and Elijah, will be sent into the world, to defend the faithful of God by divine weapons

The Father's Word, while still divine,[69]
Became a man in a virgin's womb.   330
Remaining God, He became a mortal,
Timeless God, made to live in time.
This was not done by normal law   ·
Of nature: this was God's command.
Christ took on our mortal weakness   335
To bring His strength to feeble men.
The Jews knew Him as a mortal man;
They never knew He was immortal.
They did not believe His words and signs;
Under Pilate, they crucified Christ.   340
But with His death, He ended death;
He freed the faithful from Gehenna.
He arose; He will never die;
He reigns forever, and soon will come.
He will judge mankind through fire;   345
He will raise the bodies of all men.
He will part the sinners and the just;
He will damn the evil and save the good.
You know now what the Scriptures say:
Elijah and Enoch live today.   350

Synagoga:

Where are they?

against the attack of Antichrist and to train and strengthen and prepare
the elect for war, teaching and preaching for three and a half years."
    69 As with the entrance of Antichrist (151), the importance of the
intervention of the Prophets is underscored by a change in meter; see
Introduction under "Rhythm and Music." Young (2, 384) notes that there
are numerous echoes of the Apostles' Creed and the Athanasian Creed
in their speech. A translation of the former is to be found in *The
St. Joseph Daily Missal,* ed. H. H. Hoever (New York, 1961) 1292-3; of the
latter in *The Roman Breviary,* tr. Christine Mohrmann (New York, 1964)
493-495.

Elijah:
>   We are truly they
> In whom the world's end now is come.
> He is Enoch, and I am Elijah,
> Whom the Lord has saved up to this day.
> He has come before and will come again;   355
> First Israel will be redeemed through us.
> Behold, the man of perdition[70] is come;
> He wrecks the walls of great Babylon.   358
> He is not Christ! [71]

Then they strip off Antichrist's mask.[72]   Immediately the Prophets' words convert Synagoga,[73] who says:

> We have been seduced by Antichrist
> Who claimed to be the Messiah of the Jews.
> These are certain proofs of our freedom:
> Enoch and Elijah, prophets true.

---

[70] Cf. 2 Thess. 2.3: "And that man of sin be revealed, the son of perdition."

[71] The speech ends with the half line *non est Christus*. Meyer completes the line with the emendation *sed mendax Antichristus* ("but lying Antichrist"). Other suggestions have been offered; see Young 2, 385, Michaelis 76.

[72] The Latin in this rubric (*Tunc tollunt ei velum*) is ambiguous; it could also be interpreted to mean "Then they strip off *Synagoga's* mask" or "blindfold." The Synagogue was often pictured in mediaeval art as wearing a blindfold; the same could have been true in this play. See Wilhelm Creizenach, *Geschichte des neueren Dramas* 1 (Halle, 1893) 85-86; Wilhelm Gundlach, *Heldenlieder der deutschen Keiserzeit* 3 (Innsbruck, 1899) 835; Emil Michael, *Geschichte des deutschen Volkes vom dreizehnten Jahrhundert bis zum Ausgang des Mittelalters* 4 (Freiburg, 1906) 432.

[73] See Adso 1296: "... moreover, whatever sons of Israel are found at that time, these two greatest prophets and teachers [Enoch and Elijah] will convert to the grace of faith, and from the pressure of so great a storm they will render their faith unconquerable among the elect."

We give Thee thanks, Adonai, glorious King,   365
Trinity of one Substance, Persons three.
The Father is God, as is His only Son;
Their Spirit, too, is God; and God is One.

Meanwhile the Hypocrites come to Antichrist and sing:

O summit of imperial majesty,
Your godly dignity is being robbed.   370
For two old lying teachers have appeared,
Blasphemers of the fame of your great power.
With Scripture as their witness, they advise
The Jews to shun you as the Prince of Lies.

Then Antichrist says to the Hypocrites:

When all the world gladly worships me,   375
Who dares deny to me my godhead's right?
Bring Synagoga and these old men here;
My judgment of these fools will be severe.

His servants go to Synagoga and the Prophets and sing:

Prophets of lies, and witnesses untrue,
The court of holy justice summons you.   380

The Prophets reply:

The man of evil will not entice
God's servants with ministers of vice.

The messengers then lead the Prophets and Synagoga to
Antichrist, who says to them:

An empty doctrine robbed you of your wits.[74]
You were deceived by false authority.

---

[74] I here accept the emendation *doctrina vanitatis* for the MS *proprietatis*.

I am the redemption promised to the saints, 385
The true Messiah, of whom the Scriptures tell.
Accept my faith, before it is too late,
For like a stone I crush the apostate.[75]

Then the Prophets:
You root of evil, foe of truth,
False Antichrist, corruptor of the faith, 390
Blaspheming author of iniquity,
Liar in the mask of deity.

Antichrist is aroused and says to his servants:
Behold, this blasphemy to my godhead
Will be avenged by my almighty hand.
Those who blaspheme my godly sanctity 395
Shall taste the righteous power of God's will.
As sheep for the slaughter[76] let them die,
Since they insult the faith we hold so high.

Finally Synagoga sings this confession:
Our error shames us, but now our faith is sure;
Despite all persecution we shall endure. 400

The servants lead them out and kill them.[77] While they
are being killed, Ecclesia sings:
A bundle of myrrh is my wellbeloved unto me.[78]

---

[75] Cf. Isaiah 8.14: "For a stone of stumbling and for a rock of
offense to both the houses of Israel."

[76] Cf. Psalm 44.33: "We are counted as sheep for the slaughter."

[77] See Adso 1296-7: "But after they [the Prophets] have fulfilled their
preaching for three and a half years, Antichrist's persecution will soon
begin to grow hot, and Antichrist will first take up arms against them
and kill them.... Then, after these two have been killed, he will
persecute the rest of the faithful, either making them glorious martyrs
or returning them to his side as apostates."

[78] Quoted directly from Song of Songs I.13.

When the servants have returned, Antichrist sends his ambassadors to each of the kings, singing:

> Call all the kings and regiments of saints;
> I wish to be adored in royal glory.
> The hand of God has strengthened all the world;
> Divinity has crushed its enemies.   405
> In peace each royal law is ratified,
> And God now calls his people to his side.

Then all the kings gather together from all sides with their armies, singing:

> The hand of God has strengthened all the world;
> Divinity has crushed its enemies.
> In peace each royal law is ratified,
> And God now calls his people to his side.

Antichrist says to them:

> These things have been predicted by my prophets,
> The men who venerate my name and law.   410
> This is my glory, long since prophecied,
> Which all deserving men shall share with me.
> After the victims of deception fall,
> My peace and safety[79] will encompass all.

Suddenly there is a crash of thunder over the head of Antichrist,[80] and, as he and all his men flee, Ecclesia sings:

> Lo, this is the man who made not God his strength. 415

---

[79] Cf. 1 Thess. 5.3: "But when they shall say, Peace and safety."
[80] See Adso 1297: "Learned men say that Antichrist will perish on Mount Olivet in his tent and on his throne, opposite the place where the Lord ascended into the heavens."

But I am like a green olive tree in the house of God.
I trust in the mercy of God forever and ever.[81]

As everyone returns to the faith, Ecclesia welcomes them,
singing:

Praise our God, all ye his servants,
And ye that fear him, both small and great.[82]

---

[81] Quoted directly from Psalm 52.7-8. The third line is not in the text of the play.

[82] The text has only *Laudem dicite Deo nostro.* I have added the words that follow from Rev. 19.5. See the Introduction under "Characterisation and Structure" for a discussion of the play's abrupt ending.

- Jews only active readers to Anti-Christ
- Antichrist never acting his own evil nature - solely
Unless he is led - more false prophet than deceiver.
m. bum believe that he knows that he is evil.

ADSO'S ESSAY ON ANTICHRIST

Adso's *Essay on Antichrist* (*Libellus de Antichristo*) was written in the tenth century at the request of Queen Gerberga of France. Its author was the Abbot of Moutier-en-Der; in addition to the *Essay* he wrote hymns and saints' lives and set Book 2 of the *Dialogues* of Gregory the Great into verse. He died in 992 while in Jerusalem on a pilgrimage.

Our main interest in his *Essay* is historical; as literature it is a careless piece of work. The chronology is poor; Adso adds the legend of the Last Roman Emperor almost as an afterthought, though properly it should stand at the beginning of his narrative. He makes little attempt to assimilate his sources, often quoting them almost word for word (see notes). His introduction is florid, his narrative garrulous and repetitive. The work shows no sign of careful revision. Despite all these faults, however, the *Essay* was tremendously influential throughout the Middle Ages. It served as one of the basic sources for a legend which was to have great importance in both literary and political history.

The notes to the following translation will show the extent of Adso's dependence on his sources, the most important of which were the Biblical commentaries of Haymo, Bishop of Halberstadt († 853), a theological writer and former pupil of Alcuin. The text I have translated and most of the notes are taken from Ernst Sackur, *Sibyllinische Texte und Forschungen* (Halle, 1898) 104-113. Sakur's text is reproduced in Karl Young, *The Drama of the Medieval Church* (Oxford, 1933, 1962[2]) 2, 496-500. The column numbers from Migne, *Patrologia Latina* 101, are inserted in square brackets for reference purposes.

Letter of Adso to Queen Gerberga Concerning the Origin and Life of Antichrist

[1291]   To the most excellent Queen, cherished in royal dignity by almighty God and beloved by all the saints, mother of monks and leader of holy women, to his lady Queen Gerberga, Brother Adso, the least of all her servants, wishes glory and eternal peace.

Ever since I became worthy of the bud of your pity, Lady Mother, I have always been faithful to you in all things, as if I were your personal slave. Therefore, however unworthy prayers from my mouth might be in the sight of the Lord, nevertheless I beg the mercy of our God for you and for your elder lord the King, as well as for your children's safety, that He deign to preserve in you the pillar of empire in this life, and that He cause you to reign blissfully with Him in Heaven after this life. For we believe and know for certain that if the Lord gives you prosperity and your children a long life the Church of God must be exalted and our religious order become greater and greater. I, your faithful servant, hope and pray for this; if I were able to strengthen your royal authority, I should do so must freely, but since I cannot do this, I shall pray to the Lord for your safety and for that of your children, that His grace always go before you in all your deeds, and that His glory follow you piously and mercifully, so that you, obedient to divine commands, may accomplish the good deeds which you long for, whereby the crown of the heavenly kingdom might be given to you. Therefore, because you have a pious zeal to hear the Scriptures and to talk frequently about our Saviour, and also to know about the impiety and persecution of Antichrist, as well as his power and origin, just as you have deigned to teach me, your servant, I wanted to write something to inform you, in part, about Antichrist, inasmuch as you have not disdained to hear this from me, having with you as you do a most prudent pastor, Don Rorico, the brightest mirror of all wisdom in this age of ours.

Therefore, since you wish to know about Antichrist, learn first why he has this name. This is because he will be contrary to Christ in all things,[1] that is, his actions will be contrary to Christ. Christ came as a humble man; he will come as a proud man. Christ came to raise up the lowly, to pass judgment on sinners; he, on the contrary, will cast down the lowly, glorify sinners, exalt the impious and always teach vices which are opposite to virtues. He will destroy the law of the Gospel, [1292] bring back the worship of demons in the world, seek personal glory and call himself the almighty God. Furthermore, Antichrist has many servants of his evil here, many of whom have already preceded him in the world, such as Antiochus, Nero, and Domitian.[2] In our own time also we know that there are many Antichrists. For whatever man — layman, cleric, or monk — lives contrary to justice and opposes the rule of his station in life and blasphemes the good, he is Antichrist and the servant of Satan.

But now let us consider the origin of Antichrist. The source of my information is not my own imagination or invention; rather, I found all this in written works after careful research.

My authorities say that Antichrist will be born from the tribe of Dan, according to the words of the prophet: "Dan is like a snake by the road side, an adder on the path."[3] For he will sit like a serpent by the road side, and he will be on the path to strike those who walk on the paths of righteousness and kill them with the venom of his malice. He will be born as the result of the sexual intercourse of his mother and father, like other men, and not, as some say, from a virgin alone. But he will be conceived entirely in sin, he will be engendered in sin, and he will be born in sin. At the very beginning of his conception, the

---

[1] Haymo, Bishop of Halberstadt († A.D. 853), *Expositio in epistolam II ad Thessalonicenses* (PL 117, 779): "He is contrary to Christ."

[2] St. Jerome, *Commentarii in Danielem* (*Corpus Christianorum*, series latina 75A, p. 920) mentions Antiochus, Domitian, and Nero as precursors of Antichrist.

[3] Gen. 49.17. Alcuin, *Interrogationes et responsiones in Genesin* (PL 100, 564): "Some say that through these words it is predicted that Antichrist will come from the tribe of Dan."

devil will enter with him into his mother's womb,[4] and by the devil's strength he will be fostered and protected in his mother's womb, and the devil's strength will be with him always. And just as the Holy Ghost came into the womb of the Mother of our Lord Jesus Christ and covered her with His strength and filled her with divinity, so that she conceived from the Holy Ghost and what was born was [1293] divine and holy: so also the devil will go down into the womb of Antichrist's mother and fill her completely, possess her completely inside and out, so that she will conceive by man with the devil's assistance, and what is born will be completely foul, completely evil, completely ruined. That is why that man is called the son of destruction, because as far as he can he will destroy the human race, and he will himself be destroyed at the Last Judgment.[5]

Now you have heard about the manner of his birth; hear also the place where he is to be born. For just as our Lord and Saviour preordained Bethlehem for Himself, the place where He put on humanity for us and deigned to be born, so the devil knows a fit place for this man of perdition called Antichrist, whence it is fitting that all evil will arise, namely, the city of Babylon. For in this community, which was once a famous and proud city of the heathen and the capital of the Kingdom of the Persians, Antichrist will be born.[6] It is said that he will be brought up and live in the towns of Bethsaida and Corozain; for the Lord condemns these towns in the Gospel with the words: "Woe to thee, Corozain, woe to thee, Bethsaida."[7] Antichrist will have magicians, criminals, soothsayers, and wizards, who, with the devil's inspiration, will bring him up and instruct him in every iniquity, trickery, and wicked art. And evil spirits will

---

4 St. Jerome, *Commentarii in Esaiam* (*Corpus Christianorum*, series latina 73, p. 261) calls the devil the parent of Antichrist.

5 Haymo, *ibid*.: "Who is therefore called 'destruction,' because destruction comes through him, and he himself destroys the human race." (To translate *perditio* I have used "destruction" rather than the more usual "perdition," which has no corresponding verb in English.)

6 Haymo, *ibid*. 780: "Antichrist will be born in Babylon of the tribe of Dan."

7 Matt. 11.21; Luc. 10.13.

be his leaders and eternal friends and inseparable comrades. Then he will come to Jerusalem, and all the Christians whom he cannot convert to his side he will kill by various torments, and he will place his own throne in the holy temple. He will restore the temple, now in ruins, which Solomon built to God into its original form and will circumcise himself and give out the lie that he is the son of the almighty God.

He will first convert kings and princes to his side and then, through them, the rest of the people. He will trample on the places where the Lord Jesus Christ walked, and after destroying that which the Lord has illuminated, he will then send his messengers and preachers throughout the whole world. His message and his might will prevail from sea to sea, from east to west, from north to south. He will also make many signs, great and unheard-of miracles. He will make fire come terribly from the sky, he will make trees suddenly bloom and dry up, the sea rage and suddenly become calm, natural objects change their forms, rivers change their courses, the sky tremble with winds and storms and other countless and stupendous things. He will even bring the dead to life in the sight of men, "so that if it were possible, [1294] even the elect would be deceived."[8] For when they see so many great miracles, even those who are righteous and chosen by God will wonder whether or not he is the Christ who, according to the Scriptures, will come at the end of the world.

Furthermore, he will stir up persecution of the Christians and all the elect throughout the world. He will exalt himself against the faithful in three ways: fear, gifts, and miracles.[9] To those who believe in him, he will give great presents of gold and silver. Those whom he cannot corrupt by gifts, he will conquer

---

[8] Matt. 24.24. St. Jerome, *ibid.* 231: "At the end of the world ... the miracles and portents of Antichrist will become so great that, as iniquity increases, the Christian love (*caritas*) of many will grow cold, in order to deceive, if it were possible, even the elect of God."

[9] Alcuin, *De fide sanctae et individuae Trinitatis* 3.19 (PL 101, 51): "[Antichrist will] corrupt some by flattery, some by terror, and some by miracles, so that they will worship him instead of God." Similarly Haymo, *Expositio in Apocalypsin* (PL 117, 1073).

by fear. Those whom he cannot terrify, he will try to seduce by
signs and miracles. Those whom he cannot convince by miracles,
he will cruelly torture, and put to a pitiful death in the sight of
all.[10] Then there will be such distress as never was on earth
from the time the races of men began to be even unto this time.[11]
Then those who are on the plains will flee to the mountains,
saying, "Fall upon us," and to the hills, "Cover us up," and he
who is above the roof will not go down into his house to bring
anything out of it.[12] Then every faithful Christian who is
discovered either will deny God or will perish by sword or
furnace fire or serpents or wild beasts or any other kind of
torture whatever, if he should remain in the faith.[13]

This awful and terrifying tribulation will last for three and a
half years in the whole world.[14] But then the days will be cut
short, for the sake of the elect. For unless the Lord cuts the days
short, none of the flesh would be saved.[15] Thus the Apostle Paul
has revealed the time when Antichrist will come and when the
day of judgment will appear. "But there is one entreaty we
would make of you ... as you look forward to the time when our
Lord Jesus Christ will come,"[16] he writes in the letter to the

10 This progression is followed closely in the *Play of Antichrist*. The
King of the Franks believes in Antichrist and receives gifts from him.
The King of the Greeks submits to threats of war. The King of the
Teutons is seduced by false miracles. Synagoga and the Jews are put to
death for their disbelief.

11 Dan. 12.1: "Distress shall then be, such as never was since the world
began" and Matt. 24.21: "For there will be distress then such as has not
been since the beginning of the world, and can never be again."

12 Matt. 24.16-17: "Then those who are in Judea must take refuge in
the mountains; not going down to carry away anything from the house,
if they are on the house-top."

13 Lactantius, *Divinae institutiones* 7, 17: "But those who refuse his mark
either will flee to the mountains or, when they are captured, will be put
to death by exquisite tortures."

14 Alcuin, *ibid.*: "It is predicted in the Apocalypse [11, 2] that his
[Antichrist's] persecution will burn over the earth for a space of three
and a half years."

15 Cf. Matt. 24.22: "There would have been no hope left for any
human creature, if the number of those days had not been cut short;
but those days will be cut short, for the sake of the elect."

16 2 Thess. 2.1.

Thessalonians, and explains the problem when he says "the apostasy must come first; the champion of wickedness must appear first, destined to inherit perdition." [17] For we know, since after the Greek Empire and the Persian Empire, each one of which in its own time thrived in great glory and flourished in greatest power, finally, after the other empires, the Empire of the Romans began, which was the strongest of all earlier kingdoms and had all earthly kingdoms under its dominion, [1295] and all nations of peoples lived under the Romans and paid tribute to them. [18] Therefore, the Apostle Paul says that Antichrist will not come into the world unless the apostasy comes first, that is, unless first all the kingdoms which long ago were subject to the Roman Empire secede from it. This time, however, is not yet come, [19] because, even though we see that the Empire of the Romans is for the most part destroyed, nevertheless, as long as the kings of the Franks, who possess the Roman Empire by right, survive, the dignity of the Roman Empire will not perish altogether, because it will endure in the French kings. [20] Indeed, certain of our learned men tell us that one of the kings of the Franks, who will come very soon, will possess the Roman Empire in its entirety. And he will be the greatest and last of all kings. He, after governing his kingdom prosperously, will ultimately come to Jerusalem and lay down his sceptre and crown on Mount Olivet. This will be the end and the consummation of the Empire of the Romans and the Christians. And immediately, according to the aforesaid opinion

[17] 2 Thess. 2.3.

[18] Lactantius, *ibid.* 7.15: "For it is reported that the Egyptians and the Persians and the Greeks and the Assyrians had the leadership of the world; when all of these were destroyed, the sum of things came to the Romans as well."

[19] Haymo, *Expos. in II Thess.* 780: " 'There is a power,' he says, '(you know what I mean) which holds in check [2 Thess. 2.6]' that Antichrist and which delays him, because the kingdom of the Romans is not yet destroyed nor have all the nations seceded from it."

[20] Here Adso speaks as a patriotic Frenchman and servant of the French Royal Family. The German author of the *Play of Antichrist,* of course, disagrees with him as to what nation possesses the dignity of the Roman Empire.

of the Apostle Paul, they say that Antichrist will soon be at hand, and then will be revealed indeed the "champion of wickedness," viz. Antichrist, who,[21] though he be a man, nevertheless will be the source of all sins, and the "son of perdition," that is, the son of the devil, not through nature, but through imitation, because he will carry out the devil's will in all things; because the fulness of diabolical power and of depraved nature will dwell bodily in him, where there will be hidden away all the treasures of malice and iniquity.

"This is the rebel,"[22] that is, one who rebels against Christ God and all his members, "who is to lift up his head," that is, he is risen up in pride, "above every divine name," that is, above all the gods of the heathen, viz. Hercules, Apollo, Jupiter, and Mercury, whom the pagans think are gods. Antichrist will be lifted up above all these gods, because he will make himself greater and stronger than all of them, and not only above these, but also "above all that men hold in reverence," that is, above the Holy Trinity, which alone is to be worshipped and adored by every living creature. He will lift himself up so much that "he [will] enthrone himself in God's temple, and proclaim himself as God." For as we have said above, after his birth in the city of [1296] Babylon, and his arrival at Jerusalem, he will circumcise himself, saying to the Jews, "I am the Christ promised to you, who am come for your salvation, to gather together and protect you who were dispersed." Then all the Jews will rush together to him, thinking that they are accepting God, but they will be accepting the devil. Antichrist will also "enthrone himself in God's temple," that is, in Holy Church, making all Christians martyrs, and he will be extolled and glorified, because in him will be the fountainhead of all evils, the devil, who is king over all the sons of pride.

But[23] lest Antichrist come suddenly and without warning and

21 From here to "imitation" is quoted from Haymo, *ibid.* 779. The quotations in the text are from 2 Thess. 2.3.

22 Adso here begins to explicate 2 Thess. 2.4. From this point to "Antichrist will also 'enthrone himself in God's temple'" is taken almost *verbatim* from Haymo, *ibid.* 779-780.

23 Matt. 17.11: "Elias must needs come and restore all things as they were." Apoc. 11.2-4: "But leave out of thy reckoning the court which is

deceive and destroy the whole human race at once by his error, before his arrival, two great prophets, Enoch and Elijah, will be sent into the world, to defend the faithful of God by divine weapons against the attack of Antichrist and to train and strengthen and prepare the elect for war, teaching and preaching for three and a half years; moreover, whatever sons of Israel are found in that time, these two greatest prophets and teachers will convert to the grace of faith, and from the pressure of so great a storm they will render their faith unconquerable among the elect. Then what the Scripture says will be fulfilled: "The number of the sons of Israel may be like the sand of the sea, but it is a remnant that will be left." [24] But after they have fulfilled their preaching for three and a half years, Antichrist's persecution will soon begin to grow hot, and Antichrist will first take up arms against them and kill them, just as [1297] is said in the Apocalypse: "Then, when they have borne me witness to the full," he says, "the beast which comes up out of the abyss will make war on them, and defeat and kill them." [25] Then, after these two have been killed, he will persecute the rest of the faithful, either making them glorious martyrs or returning them

outside the temple; do not measure that, because it has been made over to the Gentiles, who will tread the holy city under foot for a space of forty-two months. Meanwhile I will give the power of prophecy to my two witnesses; for twelve hundred and sixty days they shall prophesy, dressed in sackcloth; these are the two olive-trees, the two candlesticks thou knowest of, that stand before him who is Lord of the earth." Alcuin, *ibid.*: "But lest such an immense and cruel persecution, coming without warning, should overwhelm everyone when they are not prepared, the faith of the Church believes that Elias and Enoch, the greatest prophets, are going to come; through their teaching the Israelite people will be converted to the faith. When they have preached for three and a half years, they, in the very same persecution, along with the rest of Christ's faithful, will be crowned with a glorious martyrdom." Similarly Haymo, *Expos. in Apocalypsin* (PL 117, 1070).

[24] Rom. 9.27. Paul is referring to Is. 10.22: "Countless though Israel be as the sea sand, only a remnant of it will return." (The KJV translates Rom. 9.27 "a remnant shall be saved"; evidently Adso interpreted the words similarly.)

[25] Apoc. 11.7. Adso says nothing about the two witnesses' rising from the dead (Apoc. 11.11).

to his side as apostates. And whoever believes in him will receive the sign of his letter upon his forehead.[26]

But since we have discussed his beginning, let us consider the end he will have. And so this Antichrist, son of the devil and the most foul master of every malice, after he has tormented the whole world with a great persecution and tortured God's people with various punishments for three and a half years (as was said before), and after he has killed Elijah and Enoch and has crowned the rest of those who remain in the faith with martyrdom, finally the judgment of God will come upon him, as the blessed Paul writes saying:[27] "And the Lord Jesus will destroy him with the breath of his mouth."[28] Whether the Lord Jesus kills him with the power of His virtue or the Archangel Michael kills him, he will perish through the virtue of our Lord Jesus Christ, not through the virtue of any angel or archangel. Learned men[29] say that Antichrist will perish on Mount Olivet in his tent and on his throne, opposite the place where the Lord ascended into the heavens.

Moreover,[30] you ought to know that, after Antichrist is killed, the day of judgment will not come immediately, the Lord will not come to judgment immediately, but, as we understand from the Book of Daniel,[31] the Lord will allow the elect 40 days to

26 Cf. Apoc. 13.16-17: "All alike, little and great, rich and poor, free men and slaves, must receive a mark from him [i.e. the beast] on their right hands, or on their foreheads, and none might buy or sell, unless he carried this mark, which was the beast's name, or the number that stands for his name."

27 From here to the end of the paragraph is taken almost *verbatim* from Haymo, *Expos. in II Thess.* 781.

28 2 Thess. 2.8.

29 St. Jerome, *De Antichristo in Danielem (Corpus Christianorum,* series latina 75A, pp. 933-4): "There [on Mount Olivet] Antichrist will die, whence the Lord ascended to the heavens."

30 Haymo, *ibid.*: "It should be noted that the Lord will not come to judgment immediately, when Antichrist has been killed, but (as we understand from the Book of Daniel) after his death the elect will be allowed forty-five [*sic, pace* Adso] days for penance. But how much time will pass until the Lord comes is completely unknown."

31 Adso is referring to Gabriel's Prophecy of the Weeks (Dan. 9.24-27), the language of which is confusing enough to explain the disparity between Haymo and Adso as to the number of days allowed for penance.

do penance, because they were seduced by Antichrist. But[32] there is no one who knows how much time will pass, after they have fulfilled this penance, until the Lord comes in judgment; this depends on the dispensation of God, who will judge the world in that hour which He preordained for judging before the world ever existed.

There, Lady Queen; I, your faithful servant, have faithfully fulfilled your bidding and I am prepared to obey in anything else you deign to command.

[32] Matt. 24.36: "But as for that day and that hour you speak of, they are known to none, not even to the angels in heaven; only the Father knows them."

SELECT BIBLIOGRAPHY

Alcuin, *De fide sanctae et individuae Trinitatis* (*Patrologia latina* 101, 9-58; Paris, 1863).

——————, *Interrogationes et responsiones in Genesin* (*Patrologia latina* 100, 515-566; Paris, 1863).

Auerbach, Erich, *Mimesis: The Representation of Reality in Western Literature*, tr. Willard Trask (Princeton, 1953; Anchor Books 1957).

Baldwin, M. W., "The Decline and Fall of Jerusalem, 1174-1189," *A History of the Crusades* 1, K. M. Setton, ed. (Philadelphia, 1955) 590-621.

——————, "The Latin States under Baldwin III and Amalric I, 1143-1174," *A History of the Crusades* 1, K. M. Setton, ed. (Philadelphia, 1955) 528-562.

Balzani, Ugo, "Frederick Barbarossa and the Lombard League," *Cambridge Medieval History* 5 (Cambridge, 1926) 413-453.

——————, *The Popes and the Hohenstaufen* (New York, 1889).

Berry, V. G., "The Second Crusade," *A History of the Crusades* 1, K. M. Setton, ed. (Philadelphia, 1955) 463-512.

Bible: *The Holy Bible: A Translation from the Latin Vulgate in the Light of the Hebrew and Greek Originals*, tr. R. A. Knox (London, 1955).

Blondel, Georges, "Étude sur les droits régaliens et la constitution de Roncaglia," *Mélanges Paul Fabre* (Paris, 1902) 236-257.

Bousset, Wilhelm, *The Antichrist Legend*, tr. A. H. Keane (London, 1896).

Breviary: *The Roman Breviary*, tr. Christine Mohrmann (New York, 1964).

Bryce, James Viscount, *The Holy Roman Empire* (London, 1963[3]).

Carlyle, R. W. and A. J., *A History of Mediaeval Political Theory in the West* 3 (Edinburgh and London, 1915).

Chambers, E. K., *The Mediaeval Stage*, 2 vols. (Oxford, 1954[4]).

Charles, R. H., ed., *The Apocrypha and Pseudepigrapha of the Old Testament in English* (Oxford, 1913).

Chénon, Emile, *Histoire générale du droit français public et privé des origines à 1815* (Paris, 1926).

The Chester Plays (Early English Text Society E. S. 115, Oxford, 1959³).

Cohn, Norman, *The Pursuit of the Millennium* (Fairlawn, N. J., 1957).

Cooper, C. G., *An Introduction to the Latin Hexameter* (Melbourne, 1952).

Craig, Hardin, *English Religious Drama of the Middle Ages* (Oxford, 1955).

Creizenach, Wilhelm, *Geschichte des neueren Dramas* 1 (Halle, 1893).

Curzon, Alfred de, "L'enseignement du droit français dans les universités de France aux xviiᵉ et xviiiᵉ siècles," *Nouvelle revue historique de droit français et étranger* 3 Ser. 43 (1919) 209-269, 305-364.

Fournier, Marcel, "L'Église et le droit romain au xiiiᵉ siècle: à propos de l'interprétation de la bulle *Super speculam* d'Honorius III, qui interdit l'enseignement du droit romain à Paris," *Nouvelle revue historique de droit français et étranger* 3 Ser. 14 (1890) 80-119.

Fournier, Paul, "Inauguration d'une chaire d'histoire du droit canonique à la Faculté de droit de l'Université de Paris," *Revue historique de droit français et étranger* 4 Ser. 1 (1922) 249-260.

————, "Un tournant de l'histoire du droit: 1060-1140," *Nouvelle revue historique de droit français et étranger* 3 Ser. 40 (1917) 129-180.

Ganshof, F. L., *Feudalism*, tr. Philip Grierson (New York, 1961²).

Gewirth, Alan, *Marsilius of Padua: The Defender of Peace* 1 (Columbia University Records of Civilization 46, New York, 1951).

Gibb, Sir Hamilton A. R., "The Rise of Saladin, 1169-1189," *A History of the Crusades* 1, K. M. Setton, ed. (Philadelphia, 1955) 563-589.

Grene, David, and Richmond Lattimore, edd., *The Complete Greek Tragedies* (Chicago, 1959).

Gundlach, Wilhelm, *Heldenlieder der deutschen Kaiserzeit* 3 (Innsbruck, 1899).

Haskins, C. H., *The Renaissance of the Twelfth Century* (New York, 1959²).

Haymo, *Expositio in Apocalypsin* (*Patrologia latina* 117, 937-1220, Paris, 1881).

—————, *Expositio in epistolam II ad Thessalonicenses* (*Patrologia latina* 117, 777-784, Paris, 1881).

Hazeltine, H. D., "Roman and Canon Law in the Middle Ages," *Cambridge Medieval History* 5 (Cambridge, 1926) 697-764.

Heer, Friedrich, *The Medieval World*, tr. J. Sondheimer (London, 1962).

St. Jerome, *Commentarii in Danielem* (*Corpus Christianorum*, series latina 75A, Turnholt, 1964).

—————, *Commentarii in Esaiam* (*Corpus Christianorum*, series latina 73 and 73A, Turnholt, 1963).

Kingsford, C. L., "The Kingdom of Jerusalem," *Cambridge Medieval History* 5 (Cambridge, 1926) 300-319.

Kisch, Guido, *The Jews in Medieval Germany* (Chicago, 1949).

Knapke, P. J., *Frederick Barbarossa's Conflict with the Papacy: A Problem of Church and State* (Universitas Catholica Americae Studia Theologica 55, Washington, 1939).

Kurfess, Alfons, ed., *Sibyllinische Weissagungen* (Munich, 1951).

Lactantius, *Divinae institutiones* (Corpus scriptorum ecclesiasticorum latinorum 19, Vienna, 1890).

Langmuir, G. I., "The Jews and the Archives of Angevin England: Some Reflections on Medieval Anti-Semitism," *Traditio* 19 (1963) 183-244.

Langosch, Karl, *Die deutsche Literatur des lateinischen Mittelalters in ihrer geschichtliche Entwicklung* (Berlin, 1964).

—————, *Geistliche Spiele* (Berlin, 1957²).

—————, *Politische Dichtung um Kaiser Friedrich Barbarossa* (Berlin, 1943).

Lewis, Ewart, *Medieval Political Ideas* 2 (New York, 1954).

Lucken, L. U., *Antichrist and the Prophets of Antichrist in the Chester Cycle* (Washington, 1940).

March, F. A., *Latin Hymns* (New York, 1891).

Meyer, Wilhelm, *Gesammelte Abhandlungen zur mittellateinischen Rythmik* 1 (Berlin, 1905).

Michael, Emil, *Geschichte des deutschen Volkes vom dreizehnten Jahrhundert bis zum Ausgang des Mittelalters* 4 (Freiburg, 1906).

Michaelis, Eduard, "Zum Ludus de Antichristo," *Zeitschrift für deutsches Altertum* 54 (1913) 61-87.

Missal: *The St. Joseph Daily Missal,* ed. H. H. Hoever (New York, 1961).

Morrall, J. B., *Political Thought in Medieval Times* (London, 1960²).

Otto of Freising and Rahewin, *The Deeds of Frederick Barbarossa,* tr. C. C. Mierow (Columbia University Records of Civilization 49, New York, 1953).

Otto of Freising, *The Two Cities,* tr. C. C. Mierow (Columbia University Records of Civilization [9], New York, 1928).

Poole, A. L., "Frederick Barbarossa and Germany," *Cambridge Medieval History* 5 (Cambridge, 1926) 381-412.

Post, Gaines, "Two Notes on Nationalism in the Middle Ages: II. Rex Imperator," *Traditio* 9 (1953) 296-320.

Pratt, N. T., *Dramatic Suspense in Seneca and in his Greek Precursors* (Princeton, 1939).

Reeves, Marjorie, "Joachimist Influences on the Idea of a Last World Emperor," *Traditio* 17 (1961) 323-370.

Sackur, Ernst, *Sibyllinische Texte und Forschungen* (Halle, 1898).

Savigny, F. K. von, *Geschichte des Römischen Rechts im Mittelalter,* 7 vols. (Heidelberg, 1834-1851²).

Scherer, Wilhelm, "Zum Tegernseer Antichristspiel," *Zeitschrift für deutsches Altertum* 24 (1880) 450-455.

Synan, E. A., *The Popes and the Jews in the Middle Ages* (New York, 1965).

Taylor, H. O., *The Classical Heritage of the Middle Ages* (New York, 1957⁴).

Tierney, Brian, "Some Recent Works on the Political Theories of the Medieval Canonists 2: Regnum et Imperium," *Traditio* 10 (1954) 612-619.

Trilling, Lionel, "The Sense of the Past," in *The Liberal Imagination* (New York, 1950) 176-191.

Ullmann, Walter, "The Development of the Medieval Idea of Sovereignty," *English Historical Review* 64 (1949) 1-33.

————, *Medieval Papalism* (London, 1949).

Young, Karl, *The Drama of the Medieval Church,* 2 vols. (Oxford, 1962²).

Zezschwitz, Gerhard von, *Das Drama vom Ende des römischen Kaisertums und von der Erscheinung des Antichrists* (Leipzig, 1878).

INDEX

(The *Play of Antichrist* is abbreviated AX)